Paul Webb Academy: Strength Training For Goalkeepers

by Paul Webb

Published in 2014 by Bennion Kearny Limited.

Copyright © Bennion Kearny Ltd 2014

Paul Webb has asserted his right under the Copyright, Designs and Patents Act, 1988 to be identified as the author of this book.

ISBN: 978-1-910515-02-0

Published by Bennion Kearny Limited
6 Woodside
Churnet View Road
Oakamoor
ST10 3AE

www.BennionKearny.com

For Liza. Your unswerving love and support continues to inspire me to improve every single day. I love you.

Paul

Acknowledgements

It would be remiss of me to write a book and not mention a few people who have been instrumental in helping me achieve what I have kept threatening to do over the past ten years or so, and at last have finally managed to do.

I have to start with my Mum, Dad and sister, Jo. When I was young and chasing the football dream they managed to get me to games, in all weathers, fully kitted out, even if it meant missing out on other things. For that I'm sorry Jo!

More recently I've had the pleasure of working and especially learning from many amazing coaches both here, in the UK, and abroad in the US. I couldn't possibly name them all but special mention must go to John Richardson. Coach, mentor, and friend, John gave me the proverbial 'kick up the ass' you sometimes need from a coach, just at the right time.

I must thank the many thousands of clients, athletes and friends who, over the past two decades, have allowed me to 'experiment' on them all in the name of strength, fitness and health and also need to mention two people instrumental in the final development of this very book. Richard Lee and James Lumsden-Cook. Thank you just doesn't cover it.

Finally I need to acknowledge my four wonderful children. All wonderfully unique but all equally special… Shona, Nathan, Lucas and Eva, I love you very much.

About the Author

Paul Webb has been a strength and conditioning coach for over two decades.

Initially, upon leaving school, Paul was signed as an apprentice professional footballer, playing as a goalkeeper for Crystal Palace Football Club. After a successful start Paul sustained a bad thumb injury that pretty much wiped out the whole of the next season and from which he never really recovered.

Determined to help athletes in any way he could Paul began a lifelong study of his other passion: strength and athletic performance.

Fast-forward to the present day and Paul has helped hundreds of athletes - professional and amateur - from all sports improve their strength and ultimately their athleticism.

Paul can be contacted at *info@paulwebbacademy.com*

Table of Contents

1

Get Strong Of Mind, Then Strong Of Body...

This first chapter delves into the importance of a world-class mind-set. I talk a little about the science behind what separates the good from the great, talk of self-belief, show the differences between those that are successful and unsuccessful, and talk of the importance of the thoughts we have on a daily basis.

The chapter has been interweaved with stories and examples from my own experience as a young goalkeeper and some from sporting history.

It ends with a quick cheat sheet showing the main points of the chapter.

As strange and 'new age' as it sounds, before you can get a result on the outside (your body) you undoubtedly have to change the inside (your mind, or more specifically, your thoughts!).

What I don't want to do, in this section on mind-set, is get all deep, meaningful and hard-core science-y. It's really not necessary and will probably have you throwing this book on the fire for kindling.

However, there are a few things you're going to need to know if you're going to commit to substantial improvement...

Chapter 1

It's generally regarded these days; by the world's leading neuroscientists that the view you adopt of yourself will affect the way you live your life and ultimately the results you will see!

Thankfully though, it's also generally regarded that the mind-set we hold of ourselves, and our abilities, isn't fixed in stone.

As remarkable as it sounds just by making a choice and changing a thought we actually change our brain, and the way it works. FOREVER!

In science this is known as 'Neuroplasticity' and the best example I can give is the very first time you save a penalty. This could be the first time you face one or it could be the tenth, but up until that point you may feel that it's virtually impossible to keep the spot kick out. As soon as you make that first save though, even if you dive the wrong way and somehow find the ball colliding with your foot and rebounding to safety, your thought process will change.

Now you can save it!

And more importantly now you KNOW you can save it. This has a profound effect on your mind-set every time you face another penalty, even if you don't save another one!

At a neurological level your brain has changed. It has created new connections that speak to every cell in your body. Every time a spot kick is awarded against you in the future these new connections light up. They remember the save you made and the feeling you had when you saved it.

The chances of you saving another penalty increases dramatically, and sometimes it really does seem like an out of body experience as you push yet another well-struck penalty around the post!

At a really basic level, I have just described the benefit of a powerful mind-set and the effect it has on the body. You MUST understand that to not pay attention to this subject, to pass it off as some sort of 'woo-woo' fad, will leave you NEVER reaching your full potential firstly as an athlete and secondly, perhaps more importantly, as a goalkeeper!

Opportunities will be presented to you throughout your life – on the whole they will be fleeting and you'll be very lucky to see them again! The correct mind-set - knowing exactly what you want and where you are going in your life - keeps your brain on the lookout for such opportunities.

This part of the brain is known as the Reticular Activating System or RAS for short. The easiest way to explain it, is to think of it as a universal filter, blocking out most of the sensory information you are bombarded with daily.

The RAS helps ensure that what you are only focused on gets through. If this didn't happen you'd suffer from sensory overload. This is why working on the correct mind-set could be the difference between success and failure!

Self-Belief Is Developed Not Fixed

I'm sure, like me, you know the young footballer with bags of talent. I played alongside one such player in Crystal Palace's youth team. Brave, strong, fast, great in the air, sublime on the ground with both feet; without a doubt one of the best young players I had ever seen.

Unfortunately he didn't have the greatest mind-set. He always did just enough: just enough training to keep in the team, just enough ability shown on the field so he didn't get dropped, and just the bare minimum when it came to his off-field duties (we, as apprentices back then, had to sweep up, clean up, and polish the pros boots).

He was offered a professional contract, but because he thought he was worth more money he turned it down. The best player I ever saw walked away from what could have been a glittering professional career due to the way his thought process worked!

Remember that a positive mind-set, of course, doesn't guarantee you're NOT going to fail. In fact you will probably fail many more times than you'll ever succeed.

Having the correct mind-set is extremely important for dealing with those failures. Remember that failure brings you one step closer to success. You will need unswerving belief in yourself and your abilities as an athlete and as a goalkeeper to excel.

It's vital that you understand you are not born with self-belief - you develop it!

Sports history is littered with stories of athletes who have been down on their knees and considered finished, only to find a thread of self-belief enabling them to drag themselves to the top once again.

One of the greatest examples I can give you from the sporting world is that of heavyweight boxer Jim Braddock. Considered washed up, an old journeyman fighter, and all but forgotten during the great depression that gripped America during the early 20th century, he somehow pulled himself up from the pit of despair and was handpicked to give the then heavyweight champion Max Bear an easy win.

Fully expected to lose to the gifted and dominant champ, Braddock shocked Bear (who thought the bout would be so easy he didn't bother to train properly) as well as the whole of America by winning a unanimous decision and becoming heavyweight champion of the world!

Braddock had been through the hardest possible experience during the depression, barely able to work and feed his family. Yet he believed that if he worked hard, showed up to do the small things really well, when his big chance came along he would be in a position to grab it with both hands and succeed.

As a result of this incredible belief Braddock became a household name and a hero to almost every American at that time. So revered is he still, today, that a successful Hollywood movie about his life, entitled 'The Cinderella Man', was made starring Russell Crowe as Braddock.

The Difference Between The Successful and the Unsuccessful

"A man can be as great as he wants to be. If you believe in yourself and have the courage, the determination, the dedication, the competitive drive and if you are willing to sacrifice the little things in life and pay the price for the things that are worthwhile, it can be done." Vince Lombardi

It won't surprise you to discover that there is a commonality running through all successful people, just as there are commonalities running through all those who are unsuccessful. The key is to discover what the successful do and model it.

The following are four traits I've discovered that the successful do. And which the unsuccessful won't…

1. The successful do what the unsuccessful hate to do even though they may very well hate it as well – We all have things we need to do that we'd rather not. The only difference between the successful and unsuccessful is that the successful understand it needs to be done, even if they don't like doing it.

Getting up early to run hill sprints whilst the rest of the family is asleep takes courage and belief. You have to be able to let go of immediate gratification for mid to long-term satisfaction.

2. The successful take action on what they hate to do first thing in the morning before the stresses of the day take over – There is a lot to be said about getting up and getting the difficult stuff done first of all. It's not always possible though as an athlete.

For instance, vast amounts of super successful people get up really early to start work on their projects. As an athlete, sleep is a vital component of your recovery program, so if you plan to mimic an early riser like Richard Branson, make sure you compensate by getting to bed early enough.

3. The successful take action, no matter how small, every day towards their big goal – Consistency is the key to success and (unfortunately) failure! You must be very careful what you do on a daily basis, as over time, these small habits will determine whether you are successful or unsuccessful.

What are you doing on a daily basis? Is it taking you towards your end goal or away from it? Never overlook the smallest of details: it's all-important.

4. The successful never take no for an answer, they never allow a setback to stop them from succeeding – I cannot tell you how important this is… Take an early teammate of mine, Ian Wright. As a teenager he was unable to attract enough interest from professional clubs and he ended up playing for Greenwich Borough… For most people that would have been it, but Ian was made of sterner stuff and he vowed to keep playing and work as hard as he could to make it as a professional footballer.

Time passed and Ian was 21 years old, much older than most people when they get their chance. But Ian kept on producing what he needed to, and was spotted by a Crystal Palace scout.

Invited along for a trial Ian put his heart and soul and made sure that if he did fail it wouldn't be for lack of effort. Impressing then manager, Steve Coppell, he was offered a professional contract and took that same attitude into all that followed.

As you no doubt know, Ian had a hugely successful career as a player and now as a TV and radio pundit.

To Change Your Performance, Change Your Thoughts

I keep telling the athletes I train that without 100% belief in themselves they will NEVER reach their true potential!

The most important thing you can do right now is to get your thoughts working for you, not against you. You must understand that 'like attracts like', so it's important that you take responsibility for your own thoughts otherwise you WILL be affected by the thoughts of others around you.

This is why top managers like José Mourinho are in such demand. They have unswerving belief and transmit this to all their players. Could you imagine the level of performance you could attain surrounded by the players and coaching staff who all shared this 'excellence mind-set'?

That's why it's important to surround yourself with those who share the same ambitions as you. Your social group outside of football is extremely important, as we are believed to be the average of the five people we are around the most! And remember it's those little decisions we take (or which get taken for us) on a daily basis that determine if we succeed or fail!

How To Prepare Mentally

You may be too young to know of a golfer called Jack Nicklaus. He was the Tiger Woods of his day, but better!

Most golfers have a pre-shot routine they run through but Nicklaus took it a stage further. He would stand behind his ball on the tee and close his eyes. After a minute he would open his eyes, walk up to his ball, and take his shot - sending the ball flying down the middle of the fairway. When asked why he did this

Nicklaus explained that he was seeing the shot he was going to play in his mind's eye. He would call upon every experience he had, feel how he would stand, how the club felt in his hands, how the wind felt on his face, even the birds in the trees down the fairway.

He had a picture in his mind of everything around him. Then, in his mind he would address the ball, settle down, swing the club and send the ball on its way. In his mind he had already made the shot. All that remained was to actually walk up to the ball and repeat what he had visualized. And he did, time after time. Which is why he won the most majors in golf history.

This is the kind of mental preparation you need if you want to become the best goalkeeper you possibly can. This is the kind of mental preparation you need to get the best out of every training session you perform, be it on the pitch or in the gym.

You don't want to drive yourself into a frenzy here and psyche yourself out, but you do want to achieve a good mind/body connection.

Research undertaken in 2007, at the University of Lyon, showed that volunteers who visualized lifting dumbbells of different weights had muscle activation that corresponded to the load they thought they were going to lift! The heavier the weight they imagined lifting, the greater the muscle activation!

As such, you always want to have an outcome in mind. Keep asking yourself and your coaches, "What is the point of this session? What outcome are we looking for?"

NEVER undertake a training session of any kind without first knowing and understanding what outcome you are expecting. The old saying of 'practice makes perfect' is wrong! It should say 'deliberate, targeted practice makes perfect!'

Knowing the outcome of any session better prepares you for the work that's coming up. By its very nature, correct strength training is (at times) pretty brutal. To get the best results from it the correct mind-set is vitally important. This mindset, as well as the training programme, WILL stand you *HEAD AND SHOULDERS ABOVE YOUR COMPETITIORS!*

Chapter 1

You Are So Close To Excellent

Another fundamentally important part of the correct mental process is choosing the correct environment in which to express your abilities.

This includes how you train/play right the way down to the environment in which you train/play. Look at how players tend to perform better in stadiums like the Emirates over smaller stadiums like Aldershot's Recreation Ground (no disrespect intended to the fine players at Aldershot!).

Sometimes, though, you cannot control the stadium you play in so you can see why following the same mental preparation before a game is vital to get you in that place of excellence!

You only have to look at the emergence of Team GB's cycling squad to see how environment and attention to detail, even the smallest details, can, over time, make a huge difference.

In 2003, Sir Dave Brailsford became Performance Director and immediately installed a philosophy of 'marginal gains'. As well as looking at 'traditional' components such as physical fitness and tactics, Brailsford focused on more holistic elements including athlete psychology and technological developments.

Brailsford said, "If you broke down everything you could think of that went into riding a bike, and then improved it by just 1%, you will get a significant increase when you put them all together."

'Everything' included activities such as *everyone* washing their hands before any sessions to help reduce the spread of diseases (if you get the flu you cannot train)! Using this approach Team GB scored their best medal haul at the 2004 Olympics and then went on to greater success at both the 2008 and 2012 Olympics.

If you improved everything across the board by just 1% do you think you would improve? Do you think that by making small improvements you could end up improving a lot? Of course you could!

For Ultimate Success You Must Control Your Stress

A prospective new client asked me recently, what made me different to other strength coaches. Why should they spend time and money to come and work with me?

It's a great and very valid question; after all there are a huge number of strength coaches out there. Why should this young footballer (who doesn't drive and therefore needs to take public transport) travel the best part of two hours to come and train with me?

My answer shocked him, as well as his Dad and his agent (who had been the person that recommended the young footballer to me). I didn't explain how good I was as a coach. I didn't give them a list of athletes I had worked with and the great results I had got! I didn't even tell them that the training with me was different than they could find anywhere else!

I told them that when starting with an athlete my primary focus was on getting the athlete healthier and reducing their levels of stress! The healthier the athlete the more work they can tolerate and the quicker the results will come. In a nutshell, the less stress in an athlete's life the better the recovery from exercise which, after all, is just another stress!

Excess stress can, and usually does, drop all our anabolic hormones. This includes hormones such as testosterone, growth hormone, and our insulin like growth factors (a highly anabolic group of hormones which affect cell growth), all of which we need to get the best out of our training.

What that means to you, the athlete, is that if you are stressed you will always be in a catabolic state, also known as the 'fight or flight' mode. Effectively your body will always be breaking down instead of building up!

Understand that no matter where stress comes from, be it physical from training, emotional, nutritional, hormonal, or something else - the effect on the body is the same. If you seriously want to become a better athlete and ultimately a better goalkeeper you MUST get a handle on your stress levels!

In the recovery section of this book we will look at some ways we can reduce stress enabling us to train harder and ultimately get far superior results!

Chapter 1

Cheat Sheet

To wrap up part one then the best advice I can give you is that, if you are serious about becoming the best goalkeeper you can possible become (and I hope you are otherwise you've wasted your money buying this book), you *start by improving your mind-set!* The start of that process is…

Become mindful of the thoughts that continually run through your head on a daily basis – It's estimated we have over 60,000 thoughts daily but amazingly over 90% of them are the same as those we had the previous day, and the day before that…

To change an outcome you must start by changing on the inside – See in your mind's eye an event that you were part of, a great save or the day you were scouted for higher level football. Dwell on that feeling; remember as your entire body becomes flooded with those feelings of achievement, power, positivity, possibility and happiness.

You could even anchor those feelings with a so-called 'power word' – In this way those empowering feelings become associated with that word. Repeat this exercise enough and just the mention of the power word will bring these feelings flooding back through the body. This is the exact method golfer Rory McIlroy employed to help win two majors and three tournaments back-to-back this year (2014).

Follow recommendations later in this book for help with getting healthier and start to look at ways you can drop any levels of stress – Laughter is a great stress buster so please don't take yourself or life too seriously. You are meant to enjoy the ride so to speak!

Can you improve all areas in your life by just 1%? – Look at the result Team GB Cycling got through tiny, almost insignificant improvements!

Make sure you are aware of all the outcomes of all the training sessions you are taking part in – Strive to improve in each and every one of them and with that in mind let's move on to some training considerations. In the next chapter we begin to look at the role of strength training in the development of a world class goalkeeper…

2
Strength Training For Goalkeepers:
An Introduction

In this chapter we introduce the concept of strength training for a goalkeeper, the positive effect on an athlete's mind-set, and the keys to a successful training programme…

I've been saying it for 20 years now, I've mentioned it already in this book, and I'll continue to say it as long as I draw breath…

Strength is the foundation of athleticism and athleticism is the foundation of all movement. Strength is also the foundation on which you build your speed, power, stamina, injury prevention and an indomitable spirit and mental toughness.

Any training programme you undertake must, at its very core, improve you as an athlete. This is true of your warm up, your agility work, and your strength program… the list goes on.

Now, with that all in mind this next sentence is extremely important to understand – *the whole point of undergoing a strength programme is to get stronger!* You, as an athlete, must understand the intended outcome of every training session you undertake. Remember?

Although there are many types of strength - I happen to agree with elite strength coaches across the globe that really only three are applicable: *optimal strength* (which in most texts is commonly known as max strength – more on this in a moment), *dynamic strength* and *strength endurance*.

Your strength programme is intended to improve all these three areas and give you the outcome of greater strength, improved explosive power, and the ability to produce new levels of strength against fatigue.

So the intended outcome of your strength programme is not to improve your technical skills as a keeper! Any strength coach that tells you so, really doesn't understand what a strength programme is intended for.

Your Strength Programme Is Supposed To Make You Strong

I'm often amazed when I see modern 'strength programmes' that don't actually get the athlete stronger! The way you get technically better as a goalkeeper is by working on the technical aspects of goalkeeping. So, you use strength training for the reasons stated at the beginning of this section.

Your strength-training programme is better known as *general physical preparedness* or *GPP* for short. The technical work you do as a goalkeeper is known as *specific physical preparedness* or *SPP*.

GPP helps to enhance your SPP by improving many of your bio-motor abilities, such as strength (obviously), agility, speed, power, and mobility. In many ways strength is one of the keystones of GPP because, as a primary or root bio-motor ability, it has the effect of crossing over and helping so many other areas.

This will have the knock-on effect of making you a better athlete therefore improving your potential to become a better goalkeeper!

I must point out at this early stage that strength training is *NOT* bodybuilding. What you don't want to do is pile weight on indiscriminately as you get stronger. Of course, you may very well add a little lean tissue but that will be *functional muscle* that will promote your athleticism... *NOT* detract from it.

True strength training is rooted in science and is not usually found in 'workout of the month' features in this month's muscle mag!

We are always after *'relative strength'*. This is similar to training a weight restricted boxer. If our example fighter is a natural welterweight (66.5kgs / 147lbs) the last thing we want is for our training programme to take him over that weight. If we did so, our boxer would have to resort to dangerous weight-cutting methods to get back to 147lbs.

That is not our intended outcome so the training, nutrition and supplements programme has to reflect that ultimate aim. This will have an impact on the exercises we select, the amount of weight we use, the time under tension (or total repetitions), calories ingested, and more.

In many ways you reverse-engineer the process. This means that you start with a definite idea of where you need to end up - and then work backwards to where you currently are. You will then know exactly what's needed to move you towards that end goal.

That said there are exercises that naturally lend themselves to one particular group of athletes over another. Field athletes (such as discus, javelin, and the shot putt), tennis players, golfers and, of course, goalkeepers receive enormous benefits from performing an Olympic Snatch and its many variants.

The Olympic Snatch is a difficult exercise to master, mind you, and the benefit-to-risk ratio is definitely skewed towards risk for most athletes. But as the Snatch is one of the (if not the) most effective exercises for generating throwing power it is worth considering how it can be incorporated it into a goalkeeper's strength training programme. In fact, we can reduce the risk whilst losing none of the exercise's effectiveness, by switching to a kettlebell, dumbbell or even a sandbag.

The above ties into what should be the primary rule for all strength coaches. 'Do no harm'. Sadly, it is a rule that a lot of strength coaches I know personally (and whom I see online) seem to overlook.

An Holistic Approach

I always remind my athletes, especially the younger ones, that when I talk of strength training I refer (of course) to physical strength, but I also mean strength of mind, strength of character, and strength of health.

Chapter 2

Imagine the advantage that living well, hydrating and eating correctly, sleeping optimally and of course training efficiently, will give you over the competition.

Strength training can, and often is, extremely brutal and I don't want to suggest otherwise.

Accordingly, for continual progress, intensity is of paramount importance. Only 100% effort and application is tolerated with athletes that work with me because experience (both mine personally and that of countless athletes I've trained) has shown that anything other than 100% just won't cut it. In fact, a lack of complete and total effort often leads to short cuts being taken, technique becoming sloppy, excuses being made, and eventually opens the door to injury. Of course this has to be balanced with recovery and exactly where you are in your season (off season, pre-season, or in season).

The other thing that a world-class mindset will give you is world-class concentration. I can't tell you how many injuries I've seen occur in the gym that could have been avoided by just paying attention. I'm all for a great gym atmosphere and plenty of banter but when the lifts are going up it's time for business.

Remember, it's how you show up and do the little things, especially when no one is looking, that ultimately will decide the results you'll get. A huge part of an elite goalkeeping performance is maintaining a high concentration level. Switching off for just a second could be the difference between keeping a clean sheet in a hard fought 0-0 draw, or losing that same game 1-0.

That was brought home to me in a lesson I remember to this day even though it happened almost 30 years ago. When I was in my first year as a youth team player at Crystal Palace, our big rivals were Wimbledon (long before the days of MK Dons). They had a very good youth team at the time (a lot of their players went on to play for the first team) and they were certainly cut from that old Wimbledon cloth; they were tough, strong and uncompromising.

I seem to remember the away fixture ended in defeat and we were comprehensively outplayed. By the time the return fixture came around Wimbledon had been on a long winning streak and were playing with confidence. They had that certain swagger that winning football matches gives you.

We were desperate to win and despite going a goal down equalized just before half time to go in 1-1 at the break. The second half was a pulsating game of football, end-to-end, back and forth, yet we managed to take the lead to our obvious delight and especially mine.

Still celebrating as Wimbledon kicked off 2-1 down, I was slow to react as the shot came whistling in from virtually the halfway line. I tried desperately to get back and keep the ball out but could only help it, on its way, into the net. Not 20 seconds had passed since we scored and my lack of concentration had cost us the lead!

As you can see I've never forgotten the lesson those few seconds taught me and, in case you're interested, thankfully we ended up winning the game 3-2.

Remember the earlier story about Sir Dave Brailsford and his 'marginal gain' philosophy? It applies across the board to all areas of your life, but none more so that when you're about to load a heavy barbell across your shoulders for a big heavy set of box squats.

Playing any sport at an elite level takes an amazing amount of mental courage and it's for this reason that your strength training programme has to tax you mentally.

For me, lifting weights is preparing you for the good and bad that undoubtedly will happen during your life. We shouldn't be afraid of hard, brutal work. This is when you find out all you need to know about yourself.

The Key To a Successful Strength Program

What I don't want to do in this book, as I've already stated, is make it overly complex and science-y. I'm a very basic kind of guy and coach and the programmes I design are basic in nature and designed to get the maximum result from the minimum effort.

It's always worth pointing out, though, that EVERYBODY is unique and NO one training programme is perfect. An optimal training session or programme is one that must take into consideration all sorts of variables that we'll cover in a later chapter.

There are however a couple of key points that are worth bringing to your attention, although you could quite easily call them common sense.

Firstly, as we have mentioned already, *there has to be an outcome with every session.* This is arrived at by the correct execution of a plan. It's no good just 'winging' your workouts. How do you know what's working and what's not?

All sessions have to be planned. They have to move you towards the ultimate aim of being the best athlete and goalkeeper you can possibly be. All changes in the programme are planned to achieve this ultimate aim and to stop your body from adapting to the demands placed on you. This is true of warm ups, agility sessions, strength sessions and should be true even with your technical sessions.

If you were new to this type of training I would aim to change your programmes slightly every three to four weeks. This could be something as subtle as a different grip, or a change of angle, or even a different variation of the same exercise.

A more experienced athlete should change more frequently, say every two to three weeks, and elite level athletes/keepers should look at changing the stimulus every one to two weeks. All this really does depend on the individual in question, however.

I get so frustrated when I see strength coaches at clubs who write the same programme for every member of the squad regardless of their actual requirements.

Any goalkeeper new to strength training or new to training with me regardless of experience, will *ALWAYS START WITH MOSTLY BODY WEIGHT TRAINING.* I cannot begin to emphasize how important it is to have control of your body BEFORE moving on to loading with additional weight.

You have to earn the right to lift the weights!

Does that mean you don't lift weights initially? Not necessarily. It just means that until your squat pattern is optimal there is no point placing a heavy, loaded barbell on your back. Lack of a correctly grooved motor pattern, in this case the squat, would ultimately limit your end result with the loaded back squat and possibly lead to injury.

Another key consideration for me would be assessing the demands that you, as a goalkeeper/athlete, are currently facing. At the elite level you may be playing twice a week and travelling on top of that. Add a couple of days of technical work and you can see that aimlessly throwing strength sessions in may not be the best use of your time.

So, in this example, rather than plan a full-on strength session it would be prudent to perform one lift for strength and some explosive dynamic work or repetition work once a week to allow for the quickest recovery possible whilst still trying to improve.

Of course during the off-season the situation is completely different.

As part of my on-going minimalist approach (getting the biggest bang-for-your-buck) I'm a big believer in working as many muscles as possible for every repetition performed. That doesn't mean I don't isolate muscles sometimes (indeed if the athlete I'm training is recovering from injury or has imbalances, we often incorporate quite a bit of isolation work to bring them back to a place where we can load up once again).

I prefer to see athletes work large before small body parts using complex multi-joint exercises. This requires a huge degree of concentration, co-ordination, and conditioning so should be done when energy levels are high. This also leads to the biggest hormonal response and utilizes the greatest amount of energy (calories).

Understand also that as the sessions get tougher, the weights get heavier and the demands on you get tougher; you will really need to hone your rest and recovery protocols. We will talk more about this in the relevant section.

Technique is quite possibly the most important part of any lifting programme.

Poor technique is one of the major reasons trainees never reach their full potential! Endeavour to get coached in all the major lifts and never lose your technique just to lift heavier weights.

Get a good grounding in the major movement patterns - squat, hinge, push and pull, rotation, lunge and single-leg work.

Later on in this book I have included pictures showing all these movement patterns with brief descriptions. However, it would probably benefit you to get someone with knowledge of these movement patterns to run through a quick assessment with you.

Chapter 2

Cheat Sheet

In order to get stronger (and ultimately become a better athlete/goalkeeper) you will have to *commit to a progressive, well-planned, tough, and demanding exercise programme.*

Take your time to learn the lifts and be brutally honest as to your starting point. There is no point trying to squat with 100kgs on your back if you can't perform a correct body weight squat. Have a competent professional check your movement patterns or check out the pictures and descriptions provided later on in the book.

If you are new to this type of training *DON'T be in a rush to lift heavier weights.* The longer you spend learning the lifts (you will get stronger just learning the lifts, honest) the better the end result. I cannot emphasize this enough.

Work to a plan. Everything you do should be designed with improvement in mind. Always have the outcome decided before the session or sessions have taken place.

Look to train with the biggest-bang-for-your-buck! Large muscles before small; compound exercises before isolation exercises; and always free-weights over machines. If I walk into a strength and conditioning gym and it's equipped with machines (other than a couple I consider essential) I'll turn around and walk straight out! (It's happened more times than I care to mention, trust me...)

Be mindful of your ability to recover. As your volume, frequency and intensity increase you must improve your recovery and nutrition protocols. You will never reach your full potential without these essential elements in place.

Now that we've run through an introduction, our next chapter will dive straight in with some example training programs and more in depth theory on each strength training component...

3

Strength Training For Goalkeepers: The Training System

Methods are many,
Principles are few,
Methods always change,
Principles never do!

(Anon)

Chapter three is all about giving you a complete understanding into the system I use to construct training programmes. I have included examples to help with that understanding.

But before we dig into the meat of the training system, I'd just like to point out that, as the quote above wonderfully describes, there are many methods to enable a strength response.

In fact it seems that a new method is 'invented' almost every week. Unfortunately strength training is as open to the latest 'fad' as everything else seems to be! But the principles of strength training truly have stood the test of time and continue to produce outstanding results when followed.

Chapter 3

In my own experience whenever I've stripped back any fluff I've allowed myself to get caught up in and *returned to the basics*, results follow very quickly! I've personally used pretty much every type of training programme there is on my athletes, clients and myself and - without a shadow of a doubt - it's the *conjugate system* that keeps giving the best results.

Now don't get too worried about any fancy names that may appear; conjugate training is just where several different abilities are trained together during the training week. The advantage is that you can train hard all year round and still get results.

I first became aware of this method about ten to twelve years ago when all the old Soviet training manuals starting being translated. I also noticed that Louie Simmonds' famous *Westside Barbell Club* and Joe Defranco of *Defranco's Training* were using it extensively (sometimes with their own small twist) and producing some of the strongest athletes in the U.S.

The method I use the most today is slightly different to the work performed by Louie and Joe. Louie was, and still is, using the conjugate method to train mostly powerlifters. Most of his athletes are able to get to the gym and train four times a week and as a result the conjugate method is absolutely ideal.

For those other athletes who are in season, or who cannot do more than a couple of hard training sessions per week, there are limitations to this system.

To compensate for that I have followed a method for the last decade known as the 'Concurrent Method!'

All this does is take most of the benefits of the conjugate system and condense them into one workout. I really saw the benefit of this when I travelled to Edison, New Jersey, to spend some time with Zach Even-Esh founder of the *Underground Strength Gym*.

Using a minimum of equipment Zach was able to effectively perform miracles with his young athletes and he based it on a couple of simple factors...

- Turn up and do the work
- Make your weak points your strong points

Zach also impressed upon me the need to be less rigid with the structure of any training programme. Yes, the overall aim is to get stronger, but that should never take precedence over how the athlete is feeling, or any small injury that he or she may be carrying.

I ended up taking a huge number of notes during my time with Zach and the one sentence that seemed to be repeated was always to *make sure the development of speed and athleticism takes priority over strength.*

I guess it all boils down to the question, "Just how strong is strong enough?"

Of course strength is hugely important, but alongside strength the development of agility, mobility, power and speed all have to be given equal consideration.

So, effectively, the *concurrent method* allows you to flow superbly from your warm ups and movement preps into any agility work, power, strength and then hypertrophy and work capacity during one hard, effective session. This enables me to make sure that if I only get an athlete for one or two training sessions a week I have worked on every component I need to.

During the off-season and some of the pre-season I can, if I want, revert to a more traditional split where optimal (max) effort, dynamic effort, and strength endurance are spread out over the training week should I wish. In either case I mostly work in four-week blocks, which usually look like so…

Week One – *medium volume/ introductory week* (basically a learning week, checking technique, controlling the rep speed, and not going anywhere near failure on any lift).

Week Two – *high volume/base week* (still making sure technique doesn't break down under heavier loads, more explosive, still not training to failure if possible and hitting rep targets).

Week Three – *very high volume/ overload week* (let's break some records but without a breakdown in technique, going to failure acceptable this week but not encouraged as a rule).

Week Four – *recovery/back off week* (allowing for recovery and adaptation before the next four week block!) In an ideal world I'd follow this protocol all the time but as a strength coach to elite athletes I need to be slightly more adaptable, (remember we need to be extremely flexible on a day-to-day basis) something to bear in mind if you see some of my work that doesn't quite correspond to the above…

Optimal (formerly Max) Effort

To try to keep it nice and simple (which I like, a lot) all optimal effort means is to lift heavy weights over a planned time period with the aim of getting stronger. This takes a lot of commitment, focus, and mental strength, all vital components if you plan on being the best goalkeeper out there.

Within the conjugate training system this is commonly known as *Max Effort* training, but for me that gives the impression that maximal weights should be used with no consideration as to how the athlete may be feeling or what stress they may currently be under.

How strong is strong enough, remember?

I like the term *Optimal Effort* for precisely the reason that it gives you the impression that the athlete is lifting a challenging, heavy weight with fantastic technique, to the best of that athlete's ability, at that precise moment in time.

That may be heavier than the previous week or it may be slightly less. I'm not so worried just as long as - in the long run - the athlete is making progress. If we use the term max effort I've found (in the past) that the athlete can get disheartened if they are not constantly trying to lift heavier and heavier weights.

The mistakes I usually see here are the athlete unschooled in the technical aspect of the lifts, lifting within themselves so not getting stronger, and definitely lifting weights that are too heavy for their technical ability.

You'd be best advised to leave your ego well and truly out of the weights room!

Also not paying attention to rest and recovery will severely impact the results you get from this type of training. As you get stronger, your rest and recovery will need to increase as well. Never forget that.

Dynamic Effort

There is no point getting strong if you are unable to produce it when it matters, on the pitch. Dynamic training is the bridge between building strength (optimal effort) and producing it powerfully.

This type of training is used to increase the rate at which you produce force. Let me give you a quick example of what I mean...

Let's say we have two goalkeepers who can both deadlift 200kgs for one rep (1RM). Goalkeeper A takes 3 seconds to lift the bar but Goalkeeper B only takes 1 second for the same lift. This means although technically they are as strong as each other, Goalkeeper B can produce force 3 times as fast. I'd rather take a penalty against Goalkeeper A thank you very much!

I now need to make you aware of something known as the *force-velocity curve.*

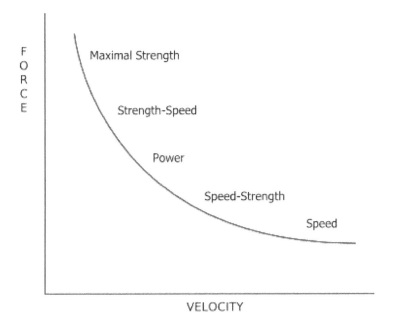

Quite simply, the curve shows an inverse relationship between force (strength) and velocity (speed). It states that the heavier you lift (force) the slower you lift it (velocity) and what that means is that - if you spend all your time at one end of the curve - the other end will weaken.

All I'm trying to point out here is that your optimal strength and dynamic, explosive strength need to be trained together for the best results.

Notice on this curve that power sits quite nicely in the middle. Lifting a heavy challenging weight with a lot of force will help you produce the necessary power. You can see that just grinding out heavy repetition upon heavy repetition could be counter-productive.

This is why I feel the concurrent method can work so well as you *DO* train for strength and explosive power at the same time. Speaking from a personal point of view it seems to make the session flow more naturally as well.

One more point, during a season I tend to spend a lot of time working with dynamic effort. I've found that when the games are coming thick and fast you will not be able to recover enough to benefit from too much optimal lifting.

The dynamic method keeps you strong, keeps you fresh, is exciting, and gives you ample recovery time as well!

Strength Endurance/Hypertrophy

These days you'll hear a lot of coaches talk about work capacity. In the past you would have heard the term conditioning or even fitness. It all means the same thing…

There is no point getting stronger, more powerful, and even slightly bigger if you can't last the pace. The best example I can give you of strength endurance is that of a boxer who is still able to produce power punches in the latter rounds of a championship fight.

A huge number of training programmes that I see, fail to take notice of the actual requirements an athlete goes through when playing his or her chosen sport.

When I was playing for Crystal Palace, every player (it didn't matter what position they played) did the same conditioning. Usually this was a six-mile cross-country run.

Even at the age of sixteen I found this strange and questioned why a goalkeeper who, back when we didn't really sweep outside the box too much, and only moved around the penalty area, should do the same as a central midfield player.

As a 'punishment' I was made to do shuttle runs after the six miles. To be fair the science of conditioning has moved on – it could still be better though!

This is also where we address the all too common issue (I'm afraid) of body fat. Far too many professional athletes, let alone footballers, carry too much body fat to be able to perform optimally at an elite level. High intensity work capacity sessions not only build a fantastic engine, they will also strip away unwanted body fat. Unfortunately, as mentioned, quite a few athletes carry too much body fat. This isn't just me preferring a more aesthetically pleasing physique, the more body fat a goalkeeper carries the harder it is to move around explosively.

Think of those shots that you're only able to parry. You have to either leap onto the ball or return to your feet for a second shot as quickly as possible. Any excess body fat will slow you down and, as you play at a higher level, these split seconds could make the difference between a save and a goal.

It's also important to mention that strength and strength endurance go a long way in assisting injury prevention. A lot of non-contact injuries occur when the athlete is fatigued.

Optimal Effort Examples

The key to getting the most out of the optimal effort approach (or any training protocol really) is to make it as highly transferrable as possible.

Remember, the role of optimal effort training is to get you as strong as possible *BUT always to enhance your performance as a goalkeeper.* It's pointless getting strong in the gym if it doesn't translate to the pitch.

For me, some of the best examples of this type of training would be strongman training and powerlifting. I also really like the Olympic lifts but would only incorporate them if my athlete was firstly physically capable and, secondly, if we had the time necessary to really learn the technical aspects of the lift. Just throwing a lift in because it looks great on YouTube isn't going to help you in the long run!

I love strongman training as a tool for developing transferrable strength and its ability to keep an athlete's interest high. As much as I love training in a gym I do appreciate it can be difficult to keep motivating yourself to go under a heavy barbell in the same facility time and time again.

Flipping tyres, dragging heavy sleds, pushing cars, loading heavy sand bags, rope work, all stuff that can be done out of the gym in the fresh air, are not only fun and challenging - they demand a different type of technique and strength you just can't replicate inside the gym.

Strongman training isn't known as the king of useable strength for nothing.

The favourite day for athletes to come and train at my previous gym was Saturday. This was outdoor strongman medley day. We would have up to twelve athletes at any one time flipping tyres, pushing my car, dragging a heavy sled and clean and pressing heavy beer kegs (or sandbags) for reps; usually against the clock.

The results these athletes got were incredible and it certainly built a strong and tight group of athletes who would encourage and cheer for everyone!

Having the right environment is essential for developing success in any area in life. Make sure your training environment supports success.

This is an actual example of how we would structure one of those sessions:

1 – Med Ball Chest Throw for distance (3 throws; average of the three recorded!)

2 – Heavy Tyre Flips (3-5 flips against the clock)

3a – Sprint 30 yards to sled (from laying on chest start position)

3b – Backward Sled Drag (30 yards)

3c – Barrel Clean and Press (12 reps; all these number 3 exercises were against the clock!)

As you can no doubt see this is a classic concurrent training session. Explosive/dynamic power (throwing med ball and sprinting), heavy optimal effort lifting (tyre flips using the heavy tyre) and strength endurance/work capacity (sprint, drag, and clean and press against the clock)

Every Saturday would see different exercises, as I'm a huge believer in frequent change to keep the results coming and preventing any boredom or adaptation for both the athlete and the coaches.

Powerlifting and Olympic lifting training could be considered more traditional strength training sessions that are carried out in the gym. If you haven't got access to any strongman type equipment they will form the majority of your exercise sessions.

Classic powerlifting exercises are the deadlift, the squat, and the bench press. I would also add the overhead press variations, bent over row, and chin ups for complete athletic development.

These types of exercises would make up the bulk of my athletes' lifting during the year, especially in the off-season.

The Olympic lifting exercises are the classic snatch, and the clean and jerk. Again, I'd rarely use them with a barbell but would use easier to coach variations using dumbbells, kettlebells, sandbags, and more.

This is how we would structure a session involving Olympic and powerlifting type exercises…

1a – Sumo Deadlifts (5-6 sets of 3-5 reps)

1b – Box Jumps (5-6 sets of 1 rep)

2a – Incline DB Press (4 sets of 6 reps)

2b – Single arm DB Rows (4 sets of 8-12 reps each side)

3a – Kettlebell Snatch (3 sets of 10-12 reps)

3b – Swiss Ball Plank (3 sets of 45-60 seconds)

As you can see this is a much more recognizable strength gym session (although some of the exercises may be unknown they are all based on the general movement patterns hinge, press, pull and rotate).

This is also an example of a full body session. Although there are times with certain athletes (especially those that lack a lot of strength in particular body parts) that I will split the body between upper and lower, generally I'll keep to full body sessions. It's important to remember, after all, that you don't have an upper or lower technical goalkeeping split, and really don't require a body part split to get world class results.

Chapter 3

Dynamic Effort Examples

Usually when you talk to someone about explosive training they immediately think of plyometric training. However, this is only one component. Also included would be speed training and Olympic lifting. To be completely honest with you any exercise could be made dynamic if the user lowered the load and moved whatever piece of equipment fast enough.

Plyometric training is probably the most misunderstood training protocol and, in this industry, that's saying something.

Originally termed 'shock training' by creator Yuri Verkhoshansky, it called for an athlete to drop from a height experiencing a 'shock' upon landing which caused an forced involuntary eccentric contraction (think about a spring compressing), before an immediate concentric contraction (think compressed spring letting go) as the athlete jumped upward.

The landing and takeoff were executed incredibly quickly (between 0.1 – 0.2 seconds) and this type of training was extremely effective in improving the speed, and power of the athlete.

Note: a strong strength base was always developed before any 'shock' training was allowed into the athlete's training programme.

Nowadays. of course, anything prescribed that uses jumping, sprinting or throwing is called plyometric and, as such, the original intention of this excellent training protocol has been lost somewhat.

That doesn't mean, however, that the modern plyometric training protocols aren't effective, it just means that any selection of the exercises, rep ranges and loads prescribed need to be monitored closely.

Speed training is exactly what it says on the tin. One thing to bear in mind is that even taking into account a big increase in an athlete's strength they are not going to get hugely faster.

The late, great speed coach Charlie Francis once said that even an increase of 300% in a muscle's strength would only elicit a 10% speed increase!

To help with speed - get strong, especially in the legs and particularly in the posterior chain (all the muscles that gym goers never train because they can't see them!) before attempting to get faster. An increase in strength will enable you to accelerate quicker… and guess what football is all about? *You got it – acceleration!*

The idea of speed training is to get faster. Dragging a heavy sled or parachute, running on sand (or downhill) will NOT help and will probably alter your running mechanics making you slower and more prone to injury in the process.

This is vitally important to understand – when asked to lift explosively or dynamically that is exactly what you need to do! What this usually means is that the load selected has to enable you to actually move quickly. I see far too many people lift, in this instance, a load that is too heavy to elicit the correct response. Don't make the same mistake.

With that all in mind this is how I would structure a dynamic session using plyometric training, Olympic lifts, and speed exercises…

1a) – Power clean (6 sets of 1-3 explosive reps)

1b) – High hurdle jumps and sprint (6 sets of 4 hurdles and 20-metre sprint)

2a) – Power Jerks (6 sets of 1-3 explosive reps)

2b) – Med Ball Throws and Sprint (6 sets of 1 throw and 20-metre sprint)

A speed session on its own could involve sets of 20, 30 or 40-metre sprints; something like…

1) 20-metre sprints (3-4 sets with 2-3 minutes rest between each sprint – yes really!)

10 minutes rest

2) 40-metre sprints (3-4 sets with 2-3 minutes rest between each sprint)

10 minutes rest

3) 20-metre sprints (3-4 sets with 2-3 minutes rest between each sprint)

The rest in this example may seem excessive but remember the outcome? We are working on speed so need to be fully rested between each sprint. *Ten, 40-metre sprints in five minutes is a conditioning session not a speed one.*

In the 'putting it all together' section of this book I will give you more examples of actual sessions I have done with footballers (and goalkeepers!) in my gym…

Strength Endurance/Hypertrophy Examples

Strength endurance (more commonly known as work capacity) and hypertrophy (more commonly known as muscle growth) usually make up most of the early training time I spend with those new to training with me.

For me, the whole point of undertaking a strength training programme with someone, is to build a solid foundation that is going to serve that person, athlete or not, for the rest of their lives.

It doesn't matter what the intended outcome of the training programme is, whether it is fat loss, muscle building, or indeed a performance-based strength programme, the better the foundation you build (in this case strength) the better the overall outcome.

This is also where we can work on somebody's weak areas and try to bring them back into some sort of balance. Again this involves us taking a longer-term view than is usually seen throughout this industry, but I've never been one to follow the herd.

A typical hypertrophy example would look something like this…

1a – Front Squats (3-4 sets x 5-8 reps)

1b – Push/Press Ups (3-4 sets x AMRAP (As Many Reps As Possible – with good technique without training to muscular failure. Don't make the repetitions too fast and stop when you feel that another rep wouldn't match the technique of the previous rep. This is known as one left in the tank!))

2a – Romanian Deadlifts (3-4 sets x 8-12 reps)

2b – Single Arm Dumbbell Rows (3-4 sets x 8-10 reps each)

3a – Dumbbell Clean & Press (3-4 sets x 6-8 reps)

3b – Swiss Ball Rollouts (3-4 sets x 12-15 reps)

A work capacity or strength endurance example could involve some sort of circuit where you have different work stations set up ready to go. The set would then involve moving between these stations performing the exercise for either time or repetitions.

Unsurprisingly this is known as *circuit training*.

Another example could involve just one piece of equipment, say a barbell, which you use for different exercises one after the other. Usually you would complete a set of repetitions on the first exercise before starting the second one and so on.

This kind of example is known as *complex training*.

Finally you could combine two or three exercises into one in an example known as *combination training*.

This is starting to get more advanced but a classic combination example would be a deadlift followed by a clean, followed by a clean and press. Each done for one repetition; you would then start with the deadlift again and so on…

The following is an example strength endurance circuit I used with a group of athletes from various sports just the other day…

1a – Kettlebell Swing (45 seconds)

1b – Recline Rows (45 seconds)

1c – Sandbag Cleans & Squat (45 seconds)

1d – Short Shuttle Runs (45 seconds)

1e – Push/Press Ups (45 seconds)

1f – Box Jumps (45 seconds)

As you can see every exercise was performed for 45 seconds and was immediately followed by a brief 15-second rest period before the next exercise was started.

After the whole circuit was completed the group had a two-minute rest before starting again and we performed five circuits in total.

Strength Training For The Younger Athlete

I'm often asked by parents of younger children at what age would I recommend they begin a gym-based strength programme. After all, they say, surely the younger they begin - the better they are going to end up?

Well herein lies the problem. I see far too many athletes, late in their teens or early in their twenties, who are unable to perform a solid push up, pull up, or bodyweight squat.

This is a huge problem and one that's born from our need to specialize our children into one sport early on *without understanding the need for general athleticism.*

When you check back into the old Soviet training methods for example, you'll see that all potential athletes and sports men and women were made athletes first *WELL BEFORE* specializing in one sport.

Kids were firstly taught how to run, jump, bound, roll and other basic gymnastic moves. After a thorough grounding in these basics they would move on to more advanced gymnastic moves, introduced to the Olympic lifts and made to participate in other sports such as swimming, football, basketball, and more.

Only when they had reached what was deemed an appropriate age were they then given coaching in the sport that they were most suited for. Sometimes this wouldn't happen until they were in their late teens.

We are far too quick to allow our children to specialize in a particular sport. I'm afraid this usually does more harm than good in the long run!

Unless your child is going to choose gymnastics as their full time sport make sure he or she gets a good grounding in all movements at an early age. They'll thank you for it in the long run.

As for the correct age a child should begin a weight training programme... that really does depend on the individual child. I've seen 12 year olds that are strong and developed enough to start and 15 year olds that aren't.

What I look for is the child being able to perform correct bodyweight squats, good quality press ups, and some sort of bodyweight row, before loaded with external weight. At the same time I'm also trying to gauge if the child has the mental strength to start to exert themselves beyond their comfort zone. For me, personally, that was at 13 years of age.

If all that stacks up, then there are no reasons why the child can't begin a well thought out strength programme. But if they are 12 or 13 years of age then the training must support them physically *not grind them into the ground.* Less is more at this stage!

Cheat Sheet

I know I've said it three or four times during this book already but it is vitally important to understand…

Each and every training session you perform has to improve you. There needs to be an understood outcome that both your coach and yourself agree on!

With that in mind each and every training session has to count. *NEVER undertake a session if you are unable to give it 100%.* When this is the case a regeneration session would be more appropriate.

Pay particular attention to your overall health. The stronger you get, the harder you train, the more demands you will place on your central nervous system, immune system, and of course your muscular-skeletal system. The healthier you are the better your results will be. Simple!

It's usually an athlete's life-style habits that compromise their performance. An example of a footballer with an impeccable attitude towards his training and lifestyle is none other than Cristiano Ronaldo. Unfortunately, even at the elite level he's an exception rather than the rule!

Technique, technique, technique.

Get strong before trying to get fast but you should put dynamic work alongside your max effort work straightaway.

What are your weak areas? Working to make them your strong areas is probably the best advice I could ever give you.

If you are a young athlete make sure you pay attention to the need for total athleticism. Spend a good amount of time running, jumping, rolling, crawling, etc. Get some gymnastic coaching; it will make a huge difference, as you get older and stronger.

The next chapter unveils what I consider to be a hugely underused tactic in the development of a world class athlete…

4

The Little Known Secret to Success

In this chapter I'm going to unveil what I consider to be the number one, and little used, 'secret' to my success…

I guess you could say I've had pivotal moments in my coaching career that have enabled me to achieve much better results in a much quicker time.

If this isn't the famous 80/20 rule in all its glory I don't know what is… (The 80/20 rule, for those who are unfamiliar, states that 80% of all results come from 20% of the tasks undertaken. This is a great help when deciding what to keep doing and what to ditch!).

A couple of these pivotal moments that spring to mind are when I first read about the old Soviet system for training their athletes, and the introduction of more mind-set coaching for my athletes and clients.

But without a doubt, by far the biggest quantum leap I've had in terms of my ability to get replicable results was when I stumbled upon the benefits of healing my clients' digestive systems…

I'm sure you've heard of the saying, "You are what you eat," but in my experience it would be far more accurate to say, "You are what you digest, transport and utilise."

A compromised digestive system basically means that whatever you eat, no matter how good for you, will not be broken down efficiently and delivered in a timely manner to where it's needed to facilitate optimal health and recovery from training…

A compromised digestive system will play havoc with your immune system and its capabilities of fighting pathogens and your recovery from the rigours of hard training. A compromised digestive system will be inflamed, and an inflamed digestive system leads to an increase in inflammation across the body. This is called systemic inflammation and is one of, if not the, leading causes of degenerative disease and injury. *So you can immediately see how important it is to have a fully functional, healthy digestive system!*

Inflammation

Most inflammation in the body begins in the gut but what exactly is it, why is it so bad for us, and how do we get rid of it?

The first thing to be aware of is that inflammation is a natural response in the body. Let's have a look at training for example.

A tough strength exercise session causes a lot of stress alongside some microscopic damage to your muscular and skeletal, central nervous, and immune systems. This places the body in a heightened state of alert, as it perceives this stress as a danger to its survival. In order to cope the body has devised a method of repair that allows us to come back healed and stronger should the stressor (training session) reappear.

Inflammation is the first phase of that process!

So that swelling, redness, tenderness and radiating warmth you feel at the site of an injury, for example, isn't an accident - it's actually the first stage of recovery.

This initial stage is known as *acute inflammation* and usually means that there is increased blood flow, which warms the area and can turn it slightly red. The affected area can also swell considerably and be quite painful, which will restrict its movement and could be claimed to be a protective measure (after all moving an injured body part could damage it further).

We are all aware of that delayed stiffness we feel a couple of days after a hard training session...

During this period white blood cells, also known as leukocytes, are cleaning up the site of the injury, mopping up the area of any pathogens, and generally overseeing the whole process.

This inflammatory process is supposed to be short and effective depending on the severity of the damage. This is why cold therapy can work so well to recover an athlete from the rigors of training. The cold helps regulate internal body temperature and stimulates immune function, both of which help to lessen inflammation and speed up recovery.

So what goes wrong? Why can something that is a natural part of recovery end up as a leading role in the vast majority of today's degenerative diseases?

Long-term inflammation, or *chronic inflammation* as it is known, is basically acute inflammation gone haywire! Usually, outside influences promote almost permanent inflammation and this has a knock-on effect throughout the body and will compromise our health.

This is because inflammation, by its own definition, has the potential to damage the body. After all, its role is to break down tissue and invade pathogens before the tissue is built back up. If the inflammation remains healthy - cells begin to be broken down!

You may very well be asking the question, "What causes inflammation to remain and cause so many problems?" The answer is quite simply 'our modern lifestyle'.

Inflammation is induced and extended by the way we live our lives and especially by:

Diet – Foods which are highly processed, high in sugar, high in chemicals and hormones, high in calories and low in nutrients *ALL* contribute to increased levels of inflammation.

Lack of Sleep – There is plenty of quality research showing that our sleep patterns are worse than ever. Unfortunately for us, this same research shows that lack of quality sleep is linked to elevated levels of inflammation.

Stress – I get it, life can be stressful. But the fact remains that no matter where stress comes from, the body deals with it in the same way. We undergo a physiological response, which not only elevates levels of stress hormones, it 'instructs' the body to begin an adaptation process enabling us to deal better with that stress should it present itself again. But, too much stress from your training programme piled on top of high levels of emotional stress could mean your powers of recovery will be sorely compromised.

Lack of Relaxation – We live in an age of deliberate distraction. These days we live our lives fully 'on the grid'. We never seem to have enough time and certainly most people take little time out of their day to just sit and be still.

Poor Gut Health – This is where a lot of the modern day problems stem from. Your gut houses the bulk of your immune system and if your gut is inflamed there's a good chance the majority of your body will be too.

It would come as no surprise to me if one, or all, of the above relate to you. Starting *ALL* my training programmes, with athletes and clients, by systematically working through the list and starting to help them put things right, has done more to help me get better results than anything else I have done in my coaching career!

That doesn't mean we don't train. It doesn't mean we aren't trying to get strong from the get go, it just means that we run through all the factors that could compromise optimal results and work hard to put them right.

Remember, we are working to a desired outcome…

This is the exact reason why I'm not a huge fan of 'miraculous' 12-week transformation programs. Research carried out at Laval University in Quebec, Canada, for example, showed that a quick loss in body fat increased the amount of circulating toxins in the bloodstream and caused a slowdown in the subjects' metabolic rates.

This simply means the subjects ended the diet with a slower metabolism, with more toxins in their bloodstream instead of being stored in fat cells, and well on their way to weighing more with more body fat than when they started. Remember, this should always be about a lifestyle change. You should strive to live correctly, like a world class elite athlete should. You need look no further than World Light Heavyweight Boxing Champion Bernard Hopkins for the ultimate example.

Hopkins has been at the elite level for over 20 years and has won multiple world titles at two different weights. He is also the oldest athlete to ever hold a world boxing title at the age of 49!

Hopkins is obsessed with details; he does the things that promote his longevity and ability to mix it with athletes half his age in one of the most demanding and dangerous sports on the planet. It's that kind of thinking you'd do well to incorporate into your armoury.

Digestive System Health

When starting with a new client or athlete, the first line of 'attack' is right here – the health of their gut. That doesn't mean we won't look at an improved diet, better movement patterns, or indeed sleep pattern, in our initial stages together, but I've found that to improve the quality of one's digestive system, and ultimately the quality of one's health, we have to look at the whole lifestyle issue to get a fully functioning healthy gut.

Our gut is home to approximately 100 trillion microorganisms; dwarfing our own cells to the extent that you could quite accurately say we are more bacterial than human.

It's this gut flora that provides us with normal gut function, comprises about 75% of our immune system, and helps regulate our metabolism. An imbalance in our gut bacteria has been linked to diseases ranging from depression to diabetes.

Several features of our modern lifestyle could be blamed for the current condition of our gut health…

- Antibiotics and other medications
- Diet low in fibre
- Diet high in processed food
- Toxins like industrial seed oils
- Stress
- Infections

As you can see, gut health is indeed multi-faceted and for optimal health you will need to undoubtedly look at all aspects of your current lifestyle. Antibiotics for example, are particularly harmful to the gut causing a profound and rapid loss, as well as diminished diversity, in the composition of gut flora. Research shows that this loss is *NOT* recovered without intervention, such as probiotic supplements.

Repairing the gut and re-establishing a beneficial gut ecosystem have helped catapult the results I can achieve with my clients and athletes like nothing else I've ever discovered.

In fact I'd go so far as to say that this alone would go a long way to improving your health and waistline.

The following are the exact protocols I currently use to help restore gut function, decrease inflammation, and increase immune function. This all leads to the ability to train harder, recover quicker, and get world-class results…

Hydration – I'm always gob-smacked at the blasé attitude most people have towards their water intake. Feelings of lethargy, indifference, muscular stiffness, etc. have all been attributed to dehydration! A great place to start is to consume a MINIMUM of one litre of clean, pure, filtered water per 25 kilograms (55 pounds approximately) of bodyweight.

To give you an example I currently weigh 98 kilograms (215 pounds approximately) so would need to consume 4 litres of water daily. Be mindful that activity and high temperatures would raise that requirement. My question to you is, "How close are you to your optimal level?"

In order to be really effective I recommend that (initially at least) you just drink water. Keep alcohol, tea, coffee, soda drinks, etc. off the menu to really reap the benefit of drinking water.

I always recommend to clients and athletes that upon rising - drink at least one (if not two) glasses of clean, pure, filtered water before doing anything else. Make this as habitual as cleaning your teeth and then start working more glasses of water into your day.

I often give clients a daily sheet to fill in which not only helps them chart sleep, diet, and activity but also how much water they've drunk. An example of this sheet is in the 'Putting it all Together' chapter.

As an addition I recommend putting a pinch of natural, clean sea salt in with your litre of water. This really helps rehydrate the body and seems to make those increased visits to the bathroom less frequent.

Nutrition – Unfortunately the average western diet these days is what I call 'calorie high – nutrient low'. Processed foods are stripped of their nutrients and pumped full of salt, sugar and God-knows-what chemicals in order to extend their shelf life and make them more attractive to us when we shop.

This has a devastating effect on our health, especially the health of our digestive system. The ultimate diet is one that obviously promotes optimal health, is free from harmful chemicals and hormones, and is 'nutrient high – calorie low'.

More on this in the next chapter, but here are my hit list of foods for digestive system health…

- Organic vegetables (especially dark green cruciferous varieties such as spinach and broccoli)
- Fermented foods (kefir, raw yoghurt, sauerkraut, etc.)
- Deep sea oily fish (high in omega 3 essential fatty acids)
- Grass fed organic meats (again for correct fat profiling and protein for repair)
- Dark Chocolate (yep, organic, at least 70% cacao but very healthy)

Avoid the following…

- Alcohol (extremely damaging to the gut)
- Sugar (will fuel the growth of 'bad' bacteria and fungal infections)
- Caffeine (can cause many issues in the gut including increased acidity and decreased mineral absorption)
- Processed foods (more on this later)

One other extremely important factor for optimal gut function is to allow our digestive system some rest and recovery as well. These days it's highly likely that, due to us snacking all day, our digestion is constantly working.

Honestly, you won't starve to death if you go more than three hours without eating – and you certainly won't go into some sort of metabolic meltdown!

The worst thing you can do for fat reduction, gut health, immune function, and more is to keep picking at your food all day. 'Stoking your metabolism' by eating little and often is a myth. It leads to stress in the gut, lowered immunity, heightened systemic inflammation and high levels of blood sugar, which leads to more calories being stored as fat.

Going longer between meals, or having a shorter window during which you take on board your daily calories, has been   shown in research to keep levels of body fat lower and extend the life of subjects (well, in this research, mice…). My only caveat with this is that if you are a professional athlete who spends 25-30 hours a week training and performing, plus a lot of additional time travelling, you will probably have to look at your nutrient timing (fancy way of saying food intake) in more detail.

We will talk more about nutrient timing in the following chapter alongside eating for optimal health and performance.

Sleep – Definitely the most underutilised component of a healthy lifestyle and absolutely free! Sleep is a powerful healer yet without an optimal amount of sleep people will crave sugar, crave coffee, and it will kill any gym gains stone dead…

Cheat Sheet

Start looking at your diet – is it high in processed foods? Does it promote gut health? Although we will go into more detail on nutrition and supplementation in the following section - what can you do right now to start the healing process?

Increase your intake of cruciferous vegetables – this family of highly nutrient dense vegetables includes spinach, kale, broccoli, cauliflower, sprouts, and cabbage.

Look at adding fermented foods to your diet – kefir, raw plain yoghurt and apple cider vinegar are fantastic for promoting gut bacteria!

What can start to be reduced or eliminated from your diet? Unfortunately optimal health and performance does come at a cost, that's why so few climb to the very top in all walks of life. Eliminating caffeine, alcohol, and sugar from your diet will be difficult but excellence is never easy!

Do you snack all day? As mentioned previously, unless you are at the elite level with elite level workloads, three meals a day will provide you with all your necessary nutrients and will be more than enough. As an added bonus this will help your digestive system and immune system function at an optimal level as well as enabling you to train harder than ever before!

Look at your hydration – One litre of water per 25 kilograms (55 pounds approximately) of bodyweight should be your initial target. How close are you to that right now? Start with a glass or two of clean, pure water upon rising and when that becomes a habit add more glasses throughout the day!

Get more/better sleep – an absolute must if you want to become the best version of yourself!

Stay tuned, for the following chapter is going to dive into the 'murky' world of nutrition and supplements…

5

Nutrition and Supplements

This chapter is all about nutrition and supplements. Before we dive in I want you to be very clear that firstly, these are the methods I use myself and with my athletes. Secondly, every person I've worked with has had to tweak my approach in some way to get the best results.

We are all unique and that also goes for the way we digest and utilise nutrients. The ultimate goal of any nutrition plan is to be able to obtain all your nutrients from a clean, natural, whole diet…

However, in the real world that's just not going to happen!

For many reasons, most way beyond the scope of this book, it's now virtually impossible to cover *ALL* your nutritional requirements from just your diet, especially if you throw daily activity into the mix.

This is where a sensible supplementation programme comes in, covering that 1 or 2% shortfall to enable both good health and optimal performance…

However, to be completely up front and honest with you it's not going to matter how hard and diligently you train if your nutrition and supplement program is not supportive of your end goals.

Chapter 5

I cannot emphasise enough how many athletes I've come across, in the past, who think (for example) that a bowl of sugary breakfast cereal is going to give them the nutrients they need to become the best athlete they're capable of being.

In order to get your energy requirements correct, achieve and maintain a correct body fat level, and maintain an optimal immune function your nutrient intake and timing *MUST* be spot on.

But, what you think is food today bears NO RELATION to the food of just a generation or two ago.

As I have just mentioned, there are a few different ways you can ultimately reach the same destination, but what I'll show you, in this section, is what has worked extremely well for all the athletes who have worked with me.

Obviously it's the theory we are interested in here. One athlete may like fish, for example, and another may not. I'll include a list of all the foods I give to the athletes that work alongside me and you can then select the actual food that most appeals to you.

The other thing to realise is that although mostly the same, we do differ in a biochemical sense. Just because one athlete can eat huge amounts of carbohydrates and stay lean and muscular, doesn't mean we all can.

There is always a bit of fine-tuning to be done. Also what may work for you at some point in your life may very well have the opposite effect somewhere down the line…

Carbohydrates were never a problem for me in my 20's; now, however, in my mid 40's they do present more of an issue and I only really consume them after a training session and then in moderation. With that in mind let's have a quick run through protein, fats, and carbs.

I cannot guarantee that a particular diet or supplement regime will work for you even if it's worked well for my athletes or even myself. Remember that every client and athlete that's stood in front of me has had to have a degree of fine-tuning for optimal results.

The Problem With Diets

I don't think any other industry bounces from fad to fad like the diet industry. It seems as if a new diet (giving you the secret that no one else has been able to uncover) is released almost daily.

On further investigation, however, you quickly notice that although the wording may indeed be different the actual diet either has you cutting calories, or cutting out fats or carbs.

The question then is… do they work? And the answer usually is yes, in the short-term they do, but give it a few weeks and then they don't. The problem then is what happens inside the body at the hormonal and metabolic level; the dieter usually ends up heavier than when they started.

The big problem with nutrition in regards to health and body composition is that it's never a stationary target we are aiming for.

Our genes (which believe it or not aren't quite as fixed as we have been led to believe), metabolism, activity level and muscle/fat ratio are always changing. Therefore our diet needs to respond accordingly.

Most diets don't take this into consideration. They also don't take into consideration someone's lifestyle, stress levels, or whether (or not) they actually like the food they are recommended to eat.

I don't think I've ever worked with someone and not had to manipulate the diet constantly! With all that said let's take a slightly closer look at what constitutes a reasonable eating plan…

The Macronutrients

All macronutrient means is 'big nutrient' (protein, carbohydrates, and fats) as opposed to micronutrient which refers obviously to 'small nutrients' (vitamins, minerals, and enzymes).

A healthy, well-rounded diet would draw from all three macronutrients but the key is obviously how much from each. Let's take a quick peek at them all…

Chapter 5

Protein: The question I wish I had a pound for, every time I've heard it over the years, would be: "How much protein should I eat?"

Firstly protein is essential. Unlike fat and carbohydrates the body doesn't really have that much of a storage facility for amino acids so it's important to take on-board a good quality protein source with each meal.

The daily recommended intake for protein is 0.8g per kilogram of bodyweight so, for example, an 80-kilogram individual would have a daily requirement of 64g.

If that doesn't sound a lot to you, you're absolutely right. You see there is a huge difference between eating just enough to prevent a deficiency, and taking in an optimal amount.

The optimal amount, however, varies greatly from person to person depending on many factors, such as activity level, age, muscle mass, state of health, physique goals, and more.

I used to believe that an athlete who trains hard would need a colossal amount of protein to help deal with the undoubted muscle breakdown that would occur, but over the last few years I have revised my thinking slightly.

I have seen studies on athletes that have shown no loss of lean tissue (muscle) on an incredibly low protein intake. So, going out and guzzling down huge amounts of meat and protein drinks, isn't actually necessary!

What I've found has worked well for my athletes is to work on two or three things initially…

i) Make sure that you take in a protein source at every meal.

ii) Make sure that protein source is of high quality, meaning that if you are eating meat it comes from an organic, as close to nature (no hormones or chemicals) source. If you take your protein from a plant based source, again you need to make sure that, as close as possible, it hasn't been exposed to pesticides, industrial chemicals and hormones.

iii) Use a quality, grass fed whey protein drink after training.

Animal protein sources provide the full complement of amino acids in the correct ratios but if you consume a diet which is free from animal products you will have to combine protein sources, nuts, seeds, beans, etc. to get the same effect.

A professional athlete, training hard multiple times a week, would probably need to consume somewhere in the region of 1.5-2g of protein per kilogram of bodyweight, giving our earlier 80-kilogram example a *daily* requirement of between 120g-160g of protein, which is much more than the 'recommended' amount of 64g!

Fat: I think it's fair to say that fat has been the dietary 'bad-boy' over the past couple of decades. Blamed for everything from heart disease to obesity a whole 'low-fat' industry has cropped up and you know what? *Heart disease and obesity continue to rise.*

Fat, even saturated fat and cholesterol, are essential to human health and without them - we as a species wouldn't have survived to the present day.

Fat makes up most of our brain, the structure of all our cells, is a precursor to our sex hormones, aids in the optimal functioning of our immune system and our hormone function, and is essential for the absorption of the fat soluble vitamins such as A, D, E and K!

However fat is highly calorically dense, more than double that of protein and carbohydrates, so eating huge amounts will cause a problem or two with the waistline…

The best advice I can give to you is to, firstly, not be afraid of fat. If you eat organic meats (and you should) eating the fat on a steak, or the skin on a chicken is going to do you more good, than harm.

Increasing your intake of oily fish is a great idea as a higher intake of Omega-3 fats has been shown to offer multiple benefits especially to the high-performing athlete! If you are a vegetarian or vegan and don't want to take fish oils then look at taking on-board flax seed oil instead.

One other point regarding fat; as paradoxical as it sounds, whenever I've had an athlete who needs to drop a little body fat (quite a few sadly) an increase in good fats, with a corresponding drop in carbs, has worked wonders.

Carbohydrates: Again, often misunderstood, it seems we can't go a day without carbohydrates either being bad for you, or actually an essential part of a well-rounded diet.

Chapter 5

The popularity of diets like Atkins, and lately the whole Paleo movement, would have you cutting off your arm if you so much as looked at a potato.

But is that attitude correct? Are carbs really that bad for you or do we actually need to eat some?

Well I think we need to look at this objectively. You would never say don't eat vegetables, berries and fruit would you? So what becomes immediately apparent is that the right carbs at the right time are indeed essential!

What you need to be aware of is that modern grains, such as breads, pastas, and rice types don't actually contain many nutrients and are generally high in calories. That kind of reflects the usual diet most of the world consumes, being what I call "high in calories, low in nutrients". This causes all sorts of blood sugar, weight, and health issues.

That doesn't mean, however, that some starchier carbs are not useful, especially when eaten at the right time…

What is apparent to me, after over two decades of training thousands and thousands of individuals both for performance and fat loss, is that carbohydrate intake is a very individual thing. Certainly it relies a lot upon both current levels of body fat and energy requirements.

An individual who needs to burn a bit of extra body fat would be best advised to carefully monitor their intake of starchy carbs, probably only eating them after a training session.

If burning body fat is not such an issue then eating more carbs wouldn't necessarily be problematic but, as I explained earlier with my own experience, you would be best advised to closely monitor your own intake.

You'll notice from the example diet later in this section that the majority of carbohydrates come from vegetables and a little fruit. There are more starchy carbs included but certainly not at every meal.

The Myth That Is Breakfast

I'm sure you've heard it said before; maybe you've said it yourself, I know I have in the past – "Breakfast is the most important meal of the day!" Is that true or is it the 'myth' I speak of in the title above?

Well, breakfast *is important* but it's not the only important meal of the day. I would say that just as important as breakfast, are your pre- and post- workout meals. That means there is a lot that can go wrong during the day so let's have a look at breakfast and why it's so important.

First a breakfast disclaimer… I'm fully aware of *intermittent fasting* in which, as a result of a 12-16 hour fast after the last meal of the day, breakfast is usually avoided altogether. There is then a phase of under-eating followed by a phase of over-eating. The process is then repeated the next day. Is it effective? I would say it depends what your goals are. If you are in a hurry to drop a bit of body fat, if you need to shift how your body uses its different energy sources then – yes - it can be quite effective.

However, it certainly isn't for everyone. I've tried it on and off over the years with varying results if I'm honest. If I have a young, athletic goalkeeper working with me who trains pretty much every day I would say that eating breakfast is going to provide much better results than not eating breakfast.

As most football training takes place in the morning, sometimes two sessions a day, I would always recommend a breakfast that provides all the nutrients and energy needed.

What makes a good breakfast then?

Let's start by looking at what the majority of people have for breakfast. Usually in a rush in the morning, the average person will either go without (usually just grab a cup of tea or a strong coffee) or reach for the breakfast cereal!

Unfortunately, if you have any dreams of being a top athlete then that kind of breakfast just won't cut it for you.

A meal high in sugary carbohydrates and milk (most breakfasts it would seem) will increase the production of a storage hormone called insulin. Insulin is responsible for the storage of nutrients in fat cells and will also contribute to an energy crash a few hours later.

Not only that but there is a real possibility of an intolerance or allergic reaction to the protein in the cereal and the milk. This will increase levels of inflammation in the body and play havoc with your ability to recover from hard training.

Are you beginning to see how this is all linked to good health?

Does that mean you can never have a breakfast cereal? Of course not. But a breakfast that contains a high quality protein source, vegetables or salad, carbohydrates from fruit or berries and some good fats from something like coconut oil would certainly, in my mind, be the choice of champions!

Definitely rotate what you eat regularly; in fact that goes for all meals. Just as if you didn't rotate the exercises you used in training, eating the same thing, meal after meal, sees the body to adapt to it and produce less of a result.

One of the very first things I do when working with a new athlete for the first time is to help them adjust to a new morning routine. They have to understand why a good breakfast is so important, and I'll show them how to make better and better choices, even if I have to teach them how to cook (true story…)

Pre- and Post- Workout Nutrition

If we decide that breakfast is the most important meal of the day then it's really the food and supplements you consume around your training sessions that come a very close second.

The first thing I'd like to make clear here is that the science behind what to eat (and when) is quite complex and in many cases contradictory. Personally, I like to keep it as simple as possible especially when you may have multiple training sessions in a day.

If you have a training session scheduled in the morning then a good breakfast (as discussed) plus a couple of important supplements (which we'll look at in a moment) will do the job nicely.

I've personally found that if I manage to get two feeding opportunities in before a training session I perform significantly better than with only one feed, but I really wouldn't lose any sleep over it! Breakfast followed by a quality carbohydrate (if body fat isn't an issue) and protein-based drink an hour or so before training will certainly hit the spot.

What is really going to help you is what you do in the hour or so after training. What you consume here will really make a difference in the way you recover from the immediate session, and your long-term results.

Straight after a tough training session the body's stores of glycogen (stored sugar) are depleted. As a result the body tends to be highly insulin sensitive (a good thing) and as such is very welcoming to a good quality recovery drink. This drink should contain both carbohydrate and protein, as both are important factors for optimal recovery and progress.

Delaying this recovery drink will mean less insulin sensitivity, which will affect the absorption of the nutrients and negatively affect the rate of protein synthesis! This is why I would always recommend a recovery drink after training followed by a meal an hour or so later…

Remaining Daily Meals

Again, without wishing to state the obvious, I don't want you to over-complicate things here…

If you are a young goalkeeper - still going to school and only training a few times a week - I'd stick to eating three good meals a day. Make sure the food comes from the supplied, approved shopping list and drink plenty of water.

Eat a large, nutritious breakfast; yes, even if that means you have to get up earlier to prepare it! Have a smaller lunch and make dinner the smallest meal of the three.

Before training, take a pre-workout drink; follow training with your post-workout drink and try not to rush when eating your food.

If you are more advanced or a professional and train a lot, then you're probably going to be better off snaking between these three meals to avoid the possibility of energy crashes.

It's really all about a bit of common sense here. There's no point eating like a professional athlete if you do two training sessions a week, or eating like a schoolboy if you max out at 14 sessions, a game, plus a 300 mile round road trip

Chapter 5

every week!

Combine carbohydrates, proteins and fats at each meal to keep anabolic materials present constantly *BUT match carbohydrates with energy requirements.* For instance, if you have a day off, drop the amount of carbs and return to normal the next day you return to action.

Let's have a quick look at an example three-meal-a-day nutrition program I did for one of my athletes (full back I'm afraid, not an heroic goalkeeper). One thing to bear in mind is that he needed to drop a little body fat so fruit was kept to a minimum and all food choices were organic:

Example 3x A Day Meal Plan

Monday BREAKFAST:	Tuesday BREAKFAST	Wednesday BREAKFAST	Thursday BREAKFAST
Nuts & Seeds	Dairy Choice	Nuts & Seeds	Scrambled Eggs
Cottage Cheese	1 TBSP Coconut Oil	Feta Cheese	1TBSP Coconut Oil
Fruit Choice	Fruit Choice	Fruit Choice	Fruit Choice
LUNCH	**LUNCH**	**LUNCH**	**LUNCH**
Green, Onion & Tomato Salad	Green Veg	Green & Tomato Salad w/ Apple Cider Vinegar	Mixed Veg
Fish Choice	Meat Choice		Meat Choice
Herb Choice	Herb Choice	Dairy Choice	Nuts & Seeds
Olive Oil	Fruit Choice	Herb Choice	Herb Choice
			Dark Chocolate
DINNER	**DINNER**	**DINNER**	**DINNER**
Poultry Choice	Potato Choice	Meat Choice	Legume Choice
Mixed Veg w/ Balsamic Vinegar	Fish Choice	Green Veg	Poultry Choice
1TBSP Coconut Oil	Green Salad w/ Apple Cider Vinegar	1TBSP Avocado Oil	Green Veg
Spices	Spices	Spices	1TBSP Organic Butter
Fruit Choice		Dark Chocolate	Spices

Friday	Saturday	Sunday
BREAKFAST	**BREAKFAST**	**BREAKFAST**
Stir-Fry Veg	Nuts & Seeds	CHEAT BREAKFAST
Nuts & Seeds	Dark Chocolate	
Fruit Choice	1TBSP Coconut Oil	
	Fruit Choice	
LUNCH	**LUNCH**	**LUNCH**
Green & Tomato Salad w/ Apple Cider Vinegar	Mixed Veg	Green & Tomato Salad w/ Apple Cider Vinegar
Fish Choice	Fish Choice	Poultry Choice
1TBSP Coconut Oil	Nuts & Seeds	Fruit Choice
	Herb Choice	
DINNER	**DINNER**	**DINNER**
Fish Choice	CHEAT DINNER	Fish Choice
Green Veg		Green Veg
1TBSP Coconut Oil		Olive Oil
Spices		Spices
Fruit Choice		Dark Chocolate

Can I also point out that this meal plan is just an example and that any change in diet, exercise routine, or other contributing factors should be undertaken at your own discretion. If in any doubt please consult your doctor or a qualified medical professional!

You can see from this example that mealtimes are very straightforward, with a lot of choice. All the food comes from the shopping list I give all my athletes which is included at the end of this section. I do prefer the fruit selection to be berries though rather than lots of apples, bananas, pears, grapes, plums and so on. Whilst I am a fan of fruit, too much, especially when you are trying to drop a little bit of body fat, could have a negative effect.

You'll also notice that I have included two cheat meals (an evening and breakfast) in this example. This is the meal when you get to eat what you want with no restrictions. It's good to have a break from time to time, just don't go overboard. You'd be astonished at how many days after a heavy Saturday night your training can be affected.

Food Choices Shopping List...

Please use this list to help you plan your shopping trips and your meal choices. If possible always try to buy certified organic BUT if you can't - please make sure that you look for as chemical free as possible and remove the fat from non-organic meat. Also make sure you wash fruit and vegetables thoroughly!

Meats: Beef | Buffalo | Lamb | Venison | Pork | Organ meats

Poultry: Chicken | Duck | Turkey | Pheasant | Goose

Fish: Salmon | Tuna | Mackerel | Sardines | Trout | Anchovy | Cod (from sustainable sources only) | Herring | Prawns | Crab | Lobster | Mussels | Sea bass

Nuts & Seeds: Almonds | Cashews | Pistachios | Brazil nuts | Walnuts | Pine nuts | Pumpkin seeds | Sesame seeds | Sunflower seeds

Legumes (only if you digest well): Black beans | Green beans | Lentils | Chickpeas | White beans | Kidney beans | Pinto beans

Dairy & Eggs (only if you digest well): Chicken eggs (white & brown) | Duck eggs | Feta cheese | Goat's cheese | Raw whey protein (if you can find) | Cottage cheese | Raw milk (if you can find) | Raw cream (if you can find)

Vegetables: Kale | Spinach | Cauliflower | Broccoli | Lettuce | Rocket | Sprouts | Swiss chard | Watercress | Asparagus | Bok Choy | Brussel Sprouts | Cabbage | Carrots | Cucumber | Celery | Garlic | Onion | Mushrooms | Peppers (all colours) | Shallots | Potato | Sweet Potato | Yam | Wild rice | Kelp

Chapter 5

Supplement Guide

The world of supplementation is a deep and murky one at the best of times and I have to confess to not being a huge fan, personally. The vast majority of the supplements you see in the supermarkets, at 'health' stores, and online, are nothing more than synthetic rubbish, and that's me being very kind to them. I can give you a great example. One of my athletes bought his whey protein supplement into my gym for us all to have a look at. The key to a good worthwhile supplement is that it's as close to a real food as possible so we were staggered to see a total of 51 ingredients included in this protein powder!

A closer examination of the ingredients with a few Google searches showed that some of these ingredients in this so-called 'natural' supplement were sweeteners, heavy metals, fertilizers, high fructose corn syrup and MSG (monosodium glutamate) which is known to be a 'exitotoxin' – over exciting cells to the point of damage or even death!

Now I'm not against using a good quality grass feed whey protein supplement, especially as a recovery drink. Whey has one of the highest concentrations of a group of amino acids know as Branch Chain Amino Acids (BCAAs), leucine, isoleucine and valine. As these amino acids are metabolized primarily in skeletal muscle instead of the liver, as all other amino acids are, they are involved in the prevention of muscle breakdown and ultimately aid in muscular repair after strenuous exercise.

That is obviously a good thing, but not so good is ingesting some sort of cheap chemical soup pretending to be protein!

We filed the 51-ingredient supplement under 'B' for bin and managed to provide a whey protein supplement that met the criteria of health first and foremost, with the grand total of three - yes just three - ingredients. As a bonus the whey came from grass fed, free range cattle! The fact remains that I'd much rather try to get as many nutrients as possible through my food, but obviously in a lot of cases that's just not possible so there are a few supplements I'd consider worth investing in.

The first one isn't really a supplement so much as a food product and that's *coconut oil.* As we've touched on briefly it's the default oil of choice when cooking for me. Extremely stable under heat and anti-bacterial, anti-fungal, and anti-viral, coconut oil really is a wonder food product and should be a staple in your kitchen cupboard.

Keeping on the subject of good fats I recommend to all my athletes an increase in the *essential fatty acid Omega-3.* You can take this as fish oil or flax seed oil. Personally I switch between the two of them from time to time. It will help decrease inflammation brought on from hard training!

Although the example meal plan shows a lot of vegetables, salad, fruit and berries it can be difficult sometimes to get enough of your greens in. A great substitute is a *quality greens drink.* Just mix with water and down it goes…

As you know already I'm a big fan of gut health and I'm sure you've heard the phrase, "You are what you eat!" It would be more accurate to say, "You are what you eat, digest and assimilate!" To help here I recommend a *good probiotic* and possibly some *digestive enzymes.* I would also add a quality *grass fed whey protein* to your list (see above).

Be aware though that, as with all of these supplements, the quality does vary - so try to make sure you get the best possible wholefood version you can.

A recent addition to my supplement hit list is *Vitamin D.* Strictly speaking Vitamin D isn't a vitamin at all but a pro-hormone, meaning it has a more hormone-like effect in the body, and is made in the skin as a result of exposure to sunlight. Never out of the news these days a deficiency of Vitamin D has been shown to lead to rickets, bone disorders, and recent research suggests a deficiency could be a leading contributor to dementia, insulin resistance and lowered immune function.

You are unable to get adequate amounts of Vitamin D from your diet so sunlight exposure or supplementation is required for this vital micronutrient especially when undergoing hard training. Vitamin D can increase levels of testosterone and fast twitch muscle fibres; both very handy during strength training! 15 minutes out in the midday sun is usually enough unless you live in more northerly areas (like me) in which case taking somewhere between 50-70 ng/ml daily will do the trick.

And that's it as far as supplements go. You could get very carried away and spend a lot of money (I know I have over the years) but there really is no need. A simple strategy always works best in my opinion in all walks of life!

One last thing regarding supplements, more specifically energy/recovery drinks. I've noticed a recent trend whereby the vast majority of athletes I train (especially the younger ones) turn up at the gym drinking some sort of energy drink. High in calories, caffeine, sugar and chemicals they have no place in your locker and cause far more problems than they solve. Get the diet and rest correct and you'll have all the energy you need.

For hydration during sessions I recommend water with a very small pinch of natural sea salt dropped in it. This will help replace not only fluids but the minerals lost through sweating, thus helping you avoid cramping. I have also had some success with coconut water. I have worked with some athletes who absolutely swear by it but if I'm completely honest I don't particularly like the taste. I can use it but only if I dilute it down with some water.

Cheat Sheet

Eat protein and fat at every meal, especially breakfast, and tailor the amount of carbohydrates to your energy requirements and body fat levels.

Most of your carbohydrates should be in the form of vegetables (especially of the dark green variety), berries, and a small amount of fruit. Make sure that you tailor your carbohydrates to your levels of activity – on those very active days eat more carbs and on those not so active days eat less.

Eat the cleanest food possible, which usually means organic. It really does make a difference especially over the long run! Worst case scenario - stay away from all processed foods and eat more vegetables – hardly anyone eats enough.

Select foods from the approved list – you have plenty of choice here and make sure you don't go shopping when you are hungry.

Supplements are exactly that… a supplement to a healthy, wholefood diet. Select the supplements that complement your normal diet and leave it at that. Don't waste your time and money on cheap, synthetic, chemically dense junk.

By all means factor in cheat meals – but keep it to two or three a week NOT two or three days a week as I've seen in the past.

Once again keep an eye on hydration levels – I know we covered this in an earlier section but it really is vitally important that you get this right. Make sure you pay particular attention to hydration levels during your training sessions.

The following chapter is going to cover what I always term, the 'forgotten' workout – rest and recovery…

6
Recovery:
The Forgotten Workout

In this chapter we are going to look at different recovery methods and just how important recovery actually is to your success.

Just like with nutrition and supplementation, you can train as hard as you want but without the correct rest and regeneration programme in place your results will be severely compromised.

The vast majority of training programs I see usually lack a coherent strategy for recovering from a session, whilst subsequently failing to allow enough time before progressing to the next one.

I can't emphasise enough how important recovery is – the demands placed on our elite footballers and athletes these days are tremendous. If you don't have a world-class rest and regeneration program in place, you will *NEVER* reach your full potential and the likelihood is, at some point, that you will break down with an injury that could quite easily have been avoided.

As your training programme, technical programme and intensity of games increases, so must your recovery.

I think, as a sporting nation, we've been a little slow in accepting the need for quality rest for our athletes. I always remember dabbling a little in Strongman competitions a good few years back and was amazed that all the European competitors would turn up with doctors, physiotherapists, nutritionists and massage therapists. We would turn up with our training partners and girlfriends.

The quality of care received by our elite athletes now is so much better, but still has a way to go in my opinion.

Recovery can be split into two sections, passive (stationary) and active (with movement). The predominant role of any recovery programme is to lower the levels of stress on the athlete. Remember, all exercise will create a stress response in the body so before you even think about what recovery programme to consider we need to look at lowering the stresses in your life...

Stress

Stress is killing you, quite literally! Recurring feelings of frustration, worry, stress and anger can cause heart rhythms to become unbalanced and disordered.

Rest and regeneration is used to counter those effects.

1,337 male medical students at the John Hopkins School of Medicine were tracked for 36 years after medical school. Those who suffered from more stress and allowed it to increase their anger the quickest, were three times more likely to develop premature heart disease and five times more likely to have an early heart attack.

Stress can come from anywhere, it can be mental or emotional stress, it can be from a hard training session (physical stress) or three losses on the bounce with indifferent performances from you personally (mental/emotional stress).

It really doesn't matter where it comes from as stress has the same effect on the body physically. Lowering your stressors so that you can tolerate stress, say from a hard gym session, is vital for continual improvement.

How do you deal with stress? Do you bottle it up inside or do you snap at the first opportunity? Learning how to handle stress is vital if you want to perform at a higher level. Moving from the Under 21 academy to first team squad will increase the pressure on you to perform every single day.

If you have no outlet for dealing with that increased stress, your performance and health will suffer.

Stress will lead to an increase in stress hormones such as cortisol. I'm sure you've heard of cortisol as it tends to get a bad rap, although in many ways it is yet another essential hormone. An increase in the production of cortisol will affect your sleep pattern, leading to more stress (and another increase in cortisol) and, ultimately, a breakdown of lean muscle.

Basically you'll get weaker, slower, fatter and more tired.

You must also understand that cortisol is affected by means other than direct stress. Drinking caffeinated drinks, taking medical drugs (such as anti-inflammatories for example), sitting in front of computer screens or T.V. - they can (and do) lead to elevated levels of cortisol.

Your lifestyle choices will affect your ability to become the best goalkeeper you can possibly be. This is the life lesson I try to impart on all the young athletes I am privileged to work with. Whether they listen or not is another matter!

Let's then have a look at some ways we can recover, both passively and actively...

Passive Recovery

I suppose the first thing to explain is what exactly passive recovery is. Quite simply, it's rest and recovery protocols performed without movement.

The ultimate in passive recovery is sleep. In my experience most people take their sleep for granted. But the recuperative powers of sleep is a book in itself. Sleep is an amazing healer and has been shown to have incredible anti-inflammatory properties (something to bear in mind if you are carrying an injury).

There are a lot of differing opinions as to the correct amount but the one thing every sleep expert seems to agree on is that the *quality* of sleep is of paramount importance.

I would say that the length of sleep is a very individual thing and can vary depending on what stress is going on in your life. However you should do all you can to make your sleep as deep and   restful as possible.

Chapter 6

Start by making your bedroom as dark as possible. Any leak of light, from the street lamps outside to electrical items in your room, will impact on your sleep quality. Good quality black out blinds will certainly help here.

Remove all electrical items from your room. You would be amazed at the research available showing how electrical equipment affects, not only your sleep, but also your general wellbeing. Stop putting your iPad or phone next to your pillow to 'track your sleep' or use as an alarm clock.

If you have to use it as an alarm then place it on the other side of the room, as far away from where you sleep as possible and turn it off.

Make sure the room is cool – not too hot and not too cold and (if at all possible) go to sleep at the same time every night. Sleep is as close to a real life wonder drug that we will ever have, and the good news is that it's not only free it carries no side effects other that helping you improve your health and function.

A close runner-up to sleep is meditation. Believe me, if you had told the eighteen year old me that I would meditate for at least 20 minutes every day when I got older, I'd have probably replied using language I couldn't possibly repeat here!

Yet regular periods of meditation of just fifteen to twenty minutes have been shown to be as effective as sleeping for a couple of hours. Some of the greatest individuals in sport and life practice daily meditation and I suggest you give it a go and see what happens.

There are many different guided meditation programs available but I mostly just sit comfortably and concentrate on my breathing. As it slows down and I relax I just allow thoughts to pass through my mind with no real attachment to them. It does take a bit of practice but I've found it to be amazingly effective.

Another passive recovery method I highly recommend is massage. A good massage therapist is worth their weight in gold!

I'm often asked what the best massage style is, and my response is, "whatever you like best…" Personally I like a really deep tissue massage. I find it best for the removal of toxins and to help decrease the recovery time after training, but it can be quite painful so I know it's not for everyone.

The last passive recovery method I usually recommend is either a cold bath or hot/cold therapy. The bath is simple. Fill up the bath with cold water and plenty of ice. Straight after training jump right in – 10 minutes should do it.

Hot/cold therapy is fantastic and can be done easily in a shower. Just immerse yourself under cold water (as cold as you can tolerate) for 60 seconds then straight under hot water (as hot as you can tolerate.) You repeat for approximately 20 minutes.

I actually find it better to finish with the hot therapy if you plan on going to bed shortly afterwards, cold finish any other time!

Active Recovery

Active recovery is the polar opposite of passive recovery. It involves movement, either just yourself, or with the help of a partner.

I'm a big fan of active recovery on off days. Just because there is no gym scheduled doesn't mean we have to do nothing. Just by getting up and moving around a little we can cut great big chunks out of our recovery time…

I suppose that the gold standard of active recovery is stretching. There are so many different types that to go through them all here would mean a chapter as long as the book itself.

Whether you opt for static stretching, dynamic stretching, or some sort of partner assisted stretching it's more about the quality of the stretching itself than the actual type. This is very important if you have someone to assist you. I saw a 'strength coach' injure an athlete by being too aggressive not so long ago.

Always start with a comfortable range of motions and never stretch into pain.

Another form of active recovery is what I place under an umbrella term of 'light activity'… This includes all those movement-based activities you could do such as power walking, light jogging, cycling, swimming, pick up games, and gentle body weight drills.

The key here is to be mindful that the outcome is recovery for the next scheduled training session, *NOT* to add to the stiffness and soreness!

A ten-minute pick up game of tennis or basketball is fine; a full match probably won't help and may open the door to injury.

Remember, the ultimate aim of recovery is to reduce the stress and micro-damage done to the body by the training sessions. Recall our big question from earlier… "What is the outcome of this next session?"

If you answered 'to improve', go to the top of the class. To improve we need to progress from the last session so we have to make sure we are in some way better able to receive the stress of that next session. The only way we are going to be able to do that is if we have recovered *AND ADAPTED* from the previous session.

All that remains for me to say on this topic is that the more prepared you are here, the more effort you put in to your rest and recovery programme, the better your lifestyle is, the better goalkeeper you will end up being… and isn't that what you bought this book for?

Cheat Sheet

Just like your warm up and actual training programme, *recovery is an essential part of you improving as an athlete* – take it seriously.

As your training becomes more advanced your recovery protocol should also improve – the majority of the athletes I've been involved with over the years always get this wrong.

Elevated levels of stress will halt your progress very quickly – try to find ways to lower your stress levels.

Sleep is a fantastic recovery tool and stress buster – what steps can you take to improve the quality of your sleep? This is absolutely vital. If you do nothing else (although you should) please make sure you sort your sleep out. Without this on board you will never be as good as you can be!

Get a weekly massage – this really is a no-brainer. You need to look at this as an investment, not a cost. Try a few different types and select the one you feel gives you the best result.

Variety in your recovery programme is vital – just as you would never do the same movement in training over and over again, make sure you try different recovery methods to help your body continually improve.

Move around on your off days – Although there are days I do no activity at all, they are rare. I much prefer to go for a walk in the woods or stretch for twenty minutes. What you do on these days will pretty much determine the results you get from all the others!

The next chapter is where we put it all together. I will show you warm ups and training programme examples for beginner, intermediate, and advanced athletes…

7
Putting It All Together

This is the chapter where, hopefully, everything begins to make sense! If you're like a lot of people, you've probably either just skimmed through the book or scrolled straight to this end section to get going on the juicy programs within.

Hopefully you've read the book and absorbed the lessons and theory contained. I've always found a little knowledge about why you're being asked to do something quite valuable.

That being said, however, you've come to this section so let me explain how it's been laid out for you... To keep things nice and simple I've split this section into three parts – beginner, intermediate, and advanced.

It's not for me to decide what category you fall into but bear in mind that I'm talking about strength training not your ability as a goalkeeper here. No matter what your age and technical proficiency if you've never lifted a barbell before - you're a beginner. I would also go so far as to say that anyone with less than two years' experience with training for strength I'd still call a beginner.

I would only classify you as advanced if you have had more than two or three years of continual strength training experience and have built a degree of physical strength that enabled you to lift at least your bodyweight plus fifty percent (probably more) in the back squat for reps.

As I said it's very difficult for me to tell you where you lie, but please try to be honest with yourself. Every athlete who trains with me does a beginner warm up, training session, and warm down, and tells me it's the hardest thing they've ever done.

The most important thing you can do is to try to get some technical instruction on the exercises included as exercise technique is vitally important especially at the beginning. The most important thing to understand when you are about to undergo any form of training, that's designed to improve you, is that you must *'get comfortable being uncomfortable!'*

Far too often I visit a gym on a regular basis and see athletes and trainees working the same exercises with the same loads they were doing a month or two ago. Whilst this may look as though they're putting in some work, in reality they aren't progressing at all. In many ways they're actually regressing and this is shown by both their physiques and their performances!

Training programmes have to be about continual improvement. Just when you think it's getting that little bit easier, in comes another stressor. I want you to remember this throughout this chapter and with the example training programmes I've included.

I'm constantly looking at ways that I can take an athlete just outside their comfort zone and am constantly watching athletes training to discover who is coping well and who's struggling a little. That's no mean feat when you may have a group of twelve to fifteen athletes in at any one time!

So it pays to be fluid when it comes to the actual taking part or the coaching of sessions. If I see an athlete who quite clearly is strolling through the planned session then I'll have no hesitation in finding ways to increase his discomfort…

Beginners

No one likes to be thought of as a beginner, especially when it comes to any physical activity. I can guarantee that when I first speak to an athlete who has expressed an interest in coming to train with me, they usually describe themselves as advanced or maybe intermediate…

However, unless the prospective athlete has spent at least two years training regularly with an elite strength and conditioning coach, then the best they can claim to be is an intermediate and most likely they are at the beginner level when it comes to their strength training.

That said I have worked with athletes, in the past, who have shown up for their first ever strength session and produced lifts that would shame an elite level lifter, but that admittedly is very rare.

The point is, once again, every athlete has to be judged on merit!

Primal Patterns

Before I start training any athlete the very first thing we do is run through the basic movement patterns. These movement patterns, often described as *Primal Patterns*, are the movement patterns we are pretty much designed to go through our daily lives performing.

They also form the foundation upon which all exercises are based, and can be described as follows:

- Squat Pattern
- Hinge or Bend Pattern
- Push Pattern
- Pull Pattern
- Lunge Pattern
- Twist or Rotation Pattern
- Single Leg Pattern

On the next couple of pages are pictures and brief descriptions of these movements. I would suggest you go through them and have your own patterns checked for any glaring faults.

Chapter 7

1. Squat Pattern

Stand with your feet a comfortable distance apart (but not too far) and, pushing out with your knees, sit back and down. Try to keep your trunk and shins as upright as possible with your spine remaining in a natural position. Keep in mind that your body type will affect how the squat looks to a degree – if you're tall (as I am) it's a lot more difficult to keep your body perfectly upright and touch your heels with your bum…

2. Hinge / Bend Pattern

Best done with a light weight (in this case a kettlebell) which you hold in front of your lap with your shoulders relaxed and back. Fold from the hips, keeping your spine neutral and push your buttocks back as if you are shutting a door behind you. Keep knees relaxed but *DON'T* squat. All the movement should come from the hips. Slowly return to the start position…

3. Push Pattern

Yep the good old fashioned push / press up. Set up with feet together and hands directly under shoulders. *DON'T* allow your elbows to flare out – you want to keep them alongside your body. Tighten everything and slowly lower all the way to the floor. Pause slightly and then drive upwards to the start position…

4. Pull Pattern

In years gone by I would use a chin / pull up to check a pull pattern but sadly not many people can perform a dead hang chin up these days. So I make do with a recline row. Lay under a secure bar, which you can just reach with an outside shoulder-width grip. Pull-back with the shoulders first and instantly drive your elbows back, bringing your chest to the bar. Pause slightly and return under control to the start position…

5. Rotation / Twist Pattern

There are many ways you can check a rotation pattern and in this example I've gone with a medicine ball chop. Set up in a comfortable athletic position with the ball raised over one shoulder. As you squat down chop the ball across the body to the outside of the opposite knee. Rotate your trunk as you chop, and return to the start position. Repeat on the other side…

6. Lunge Pattern

I usually utilize the reverse lunge to check this pattern, as generally it's the version that causes the fewest technical issues! Stand tall and reach back with one foot. As you plant the rear foot, make sure the front foot is completely flat on the ground. *DON'T* hyperextend the lower back (lean back too far) and drive off the front foot to return to the start position. Repeat on the other side...

7. Single Leg Pattern

If you think about it, most movement (especially in sport) involves a great deal of time on one leg, so it stands to reason to improve an athlete's ability in this position. Select something flat to stand on with one leg and slowly lower into a single leg squat. Go down as far as is comfortable, pause briefly and return to the start position. Repeat on the other side…

Chapter 7

Once I'm satisfied the basic movements are understood and are able to be performed with no real stress, and I really don't want you to get too caught up at this stage as this is something that can be tweaked as we progress, we move on to beginning a four-week training program (in this example we've based our weekly program on match day being Saturday…)

As with *ALL* my exercise programs it all begins with a warm up. I recommend that you never skimp on the warm up as I see so many athletes try to do.

Long gone are the days when you can expect to compete as an elite athlete and neglect any part of the package. Many moons ago when I was playing for Crystal Palace youth team and reserves, the warm up on training days was basically a small run and a couple of drills. Match day warm ups were even worse – players lined up on the edge of the penalty box and fired shots at my goal, with the occasional cross!

I remember playing Southampton at their famous old ground 'The Dell' and as I came out for my 'shot-stopping' warm up caught a glimpse of a couple of their players laying down on the pitch watching the world go by.

How times have changed…

Nowadays players run through a fully comprehensive warm up program *BEFORE* any match and, although I do believe it could be better, it certainly is a world away from my experiences.

There are many different reasons to take a warm up seriously: prepping muscles for the work to come, increasing blood flow, stimulating the *CNS*, increasing your range of movement, prepping the athlete mentally, but *FUNDAMENTALLY* I look at the warm up as injury prevention.

By no stretch of the imagination will a warm up prevent all injuries but certainly it plays a huge role in lessening the chances of injury happening.

Let's have a look at some of the warm ups I use with my athletes…

Beginners Warm Ups

These warm ups can be mixed and matched as you see fit although I tend to always use the SMR and Resistance Band pair with all warm ups. Their benefit has been proven 'in the trenches' over the last fifteen years or so…

Self Myofascial Release Warm Up

The term 'self myofascial release' or *SMR* refers to what is happening during these exercises. The simplest way to explain it is to compare it to deep tissue massage. Years of training causes scar tissue and 'knots' in the muscle tissue and surrounding fascia to develop which, if not treated, will inhibit a person's range of movement and contractile potential (how well the muscle squeezes) in the muscle itself.

Using tools such as firm tennis balls, golf balls and foam rollers can stop this from happening therefore ultimately improving your results.

Chapter 7

1. Tennis Ball Foot Roll

Place a firm tennis ball or, if you are braver, golf ball on the floor and roll your shoeless sole over the ball as firmly as you can. Make sure you cover the base of your foot completely and if a specific spot is particularly tender spend a bit more time there. Repeat on the other foot for 30-60 seconds each side…

2. Piriformis / Glute Roll

Place one buttock on the roller and lean back with the same side's hand on the floor. Put the same side's foot up on the opposite knee and gently roll out, backwards and forwards over the entire buttock. Repeat on the other buttock for 30-60 seconds each side…

3. I.T. Band Roll

One that brings a tear to the eye of the very bravest, the Iliotibial Band is a sheath of fascia that runs between the side of the hip to the side of the knee and is often extremely tight! In some people, no amount of rolling seems to help, but personally I've found it very useful. Place a roller under the side of your hip and roll down to just above the knee. Be careful and repeat on the other leg for 30-60 seconds each side…

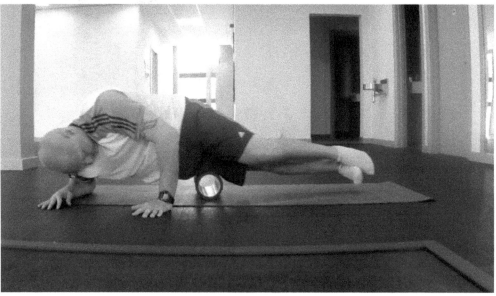

4. Quadricep Roll

Although you could roll both quads together you get much better results by doing each separately. Place one thigh on a roller, bend your knee stretching the quad slightly and roll up and down making sure to cover the whole of the thigh. Repeat on the other quad (30-60 seconds each side)…

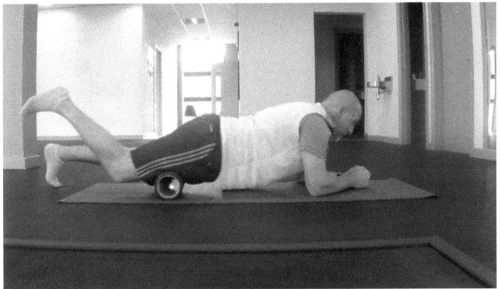

5. Adductor Roll

Another one for the brave, this is a tricky movement to master and usually works a very tight group of muscles. Lie on an angled roller alongside the inside of the knee and roll towards the groin. Repeat on the other leg for 30-60 seconds each side…

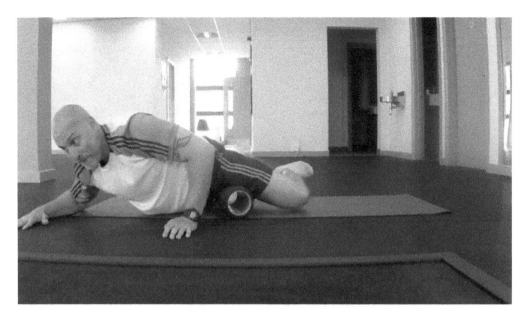

6. Calf Roll

Again one that can be done separately or together. Place a calf on a roller and roll from the heel to before the knee. Repeat on the other calf for 30-60 seconds each side…

7. Back Roll

Lie with roller between shoulder blades and arms folded across chest. Brace abdominals slightly and lift hips off floor. Slowly roll up and down the roller from below the neck to the lower back and concentrate on any spots that are particularly tight or sore. Continue for between 30 and 60 seconds...

Resistance Band Warm Up

Another of my 'essential' warm ups, a resistance band is a fantastic bit of kit which will help you move with varying levels of resistance, depending on the thickness of band selected, through a good range of movement. In the following examples I place a huge degree of importance on retraction (pulling) and external rotation. This is due to our current lifestyle of sitting (mostly) with our back flexed (rounded) and our shoulders rotated internally!

1. Prone Band Pull-Apart

Grab a band with slight tension at chest level with both arms straight out in front of you and palms facing down (prone). Bring the hands together and keeping your arms straight pull your hands apart squeezing your shoulder blades together. It's extremely important to make sure your posture is upright and your shoulders stay relaxed and down. Return to the start point and repeat for 10-20 reps…

2. Supine Band Pull-Apart

Exactly the same technique as the prone version EXCEPT that your palms now face upwards (supine!) Again repeat for 10-20 reps…

3. Angled Band Pull Apart

With the same band return your hands to the prone position and place them by the side of one hip. Pull upwards and across the body extending the arm fully. Again stay relaxed with good posture as you return to the start position. Swap to the opposite side and repeat for 10-20 reps each…

4. Band Dislocations

With hands on the band just outside shoulder width, and the resistance band pulled slightly taught, lift the band up and over your head and right down your back to the top of your buttocks keeping your arms straight. Return to the start position. Repeat for 10-20 reps…

5. Band Rear Press

Performed exactly like a behind the neck press, pull the band apart at the start point behind your neck and slowly press the band upwards. Pause for a second at the top and then return to the start point. Repeat for 10-20 reps…

6. Band Face Pulls

Hook a band up at above head height and stand back holding the band in both hands at arm's length. Again keep a good posture as you pull your elbows back and the band just under your chin. Repeat for 10-20 reps…

7. Band Face Pulls with External Rotation

Perform a face pull as previously *BUT* in the pulled back midpoint of the repetition rotate from the shoulder lifting the arms straight up. At the top of the rotation your hands should be directly above your elbows. Return to the starting position and repeat for 10-20 reps...

Dynamic Mat Work Warm Up

To be completely honest with you the type of warm up I have my athletes perform will depend on a number of factors.

I'll always look to do some sort of SMR and resistance band warm up and then usually I'll chop and change depending on how advanced the group I'm training is, what the requirements for the session are, how much space is available to warm up in, etc.

One common theme though is I like *ALL* the athletes to warm up dynamically as a rule. It's not that I have anything against static warm ups (a static hip flexor stretch can really help with squat depth for example), but as we are going to train dynamically I like the added benefit of dynamic movement from the get-go!

Let's have a look at a dynamic mat work warm up…

1. Single Leg Swings

Lay flat on a mat with both legs straight and your toes pointing up (dorsiflexed). Keeping your hips straight and your lower back from arching, lift one leg straight up as high as you can *WITHOUT* going too deep into the stretch. Return to the start point and repeat with the same leg. As you perform more repetitions your range of movement should increase, proving the benefit of the dynamic nature of the warm up. Perform 10-15 reps on one leg then repeat on the other…

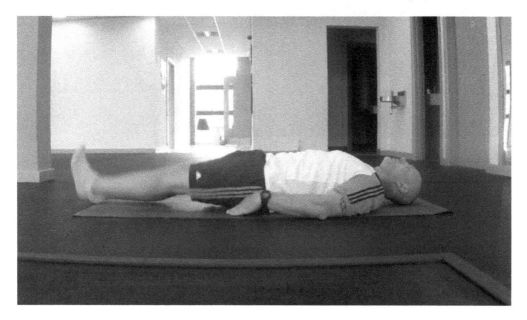

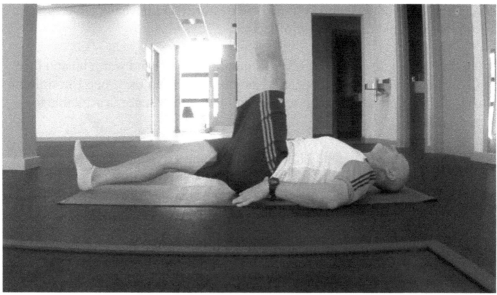

2. Hip Bridge

Keeping knees and feet slightly apart, bend the knees and place your feet on the floor comfortably away from your buttocks. The further away the harder the movement! Drive through your heels *ONLY* and lift your hips high without going into hyperextension. Squeeze the buttocks and hamstrings hard, hold for a count of two seconds and lower slowly to the starting position. Repeat for 10-15 reps…

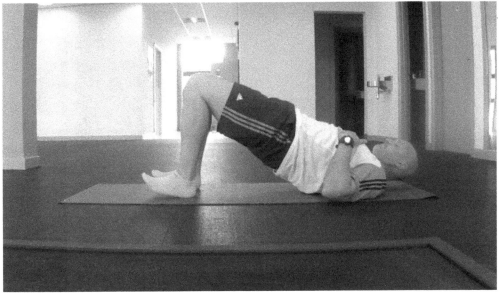

3. Single Leg Hip Bridge

Set up exactly as the previous movement but this time lift one leg off the floor. You are performing a similar hip bridge but, this time, have more of a stability issue to deal with. Drive through the single heel, go as high as possible with no hyperextension, and squeeze buttock and hamstring. Return to the start position for all reps on that side then change. Perform 5-6 reps each side...

4. Iron Cross

Again set up in the hip bridge position but this time stretch your arms out straight and lift your feet off the floor. Keeping your arms straight and shoulders on the floor drop your legs (kept together) down to one side. As you do this look the other way. Repeat the other side for 10-12 reps each side...

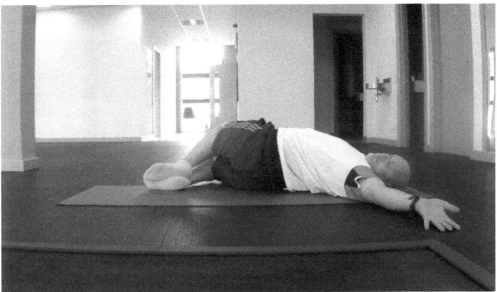

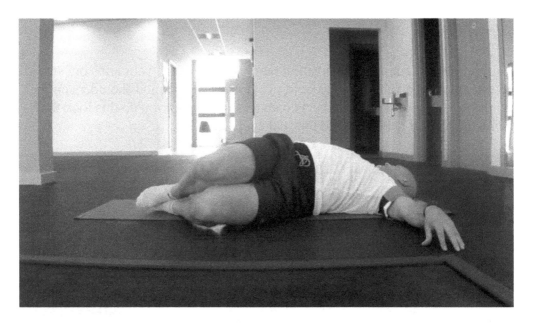

5. Prone Scorpion

As the title suggests, begin by laying prone (face down) on the floor. Spread your arms out straight to the sides and keeping your shoulders down take one foot and reach up and over the body trying to touch down as close as possible to the opposite hand. Alternate sides for between 5 – 10 repetitions…

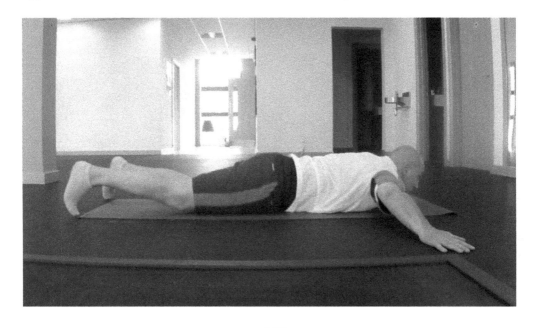

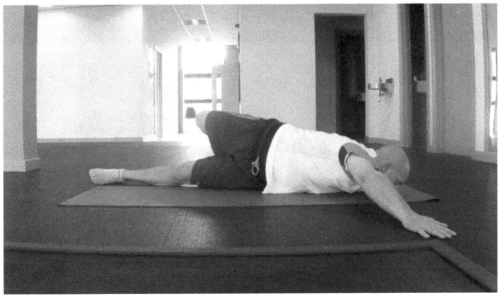

6. Rocking 'Frog' Stretch

Sit in a frog-like position with knees spread and feet slightly closer together. Be very careful here as you 'rock' back towards your ankles - holding for a brief count - before 'rocking' forwards and dropping your hips, again holding for a brief count. Increase the stretch as you go, repeating for 5 – 10 repetitions...

7. Child Pose into Abdominal Stretch

Begin by sitting back onto your heels and then 'scoop' your chest along the floor finally extending your lower back and stretching abdominal muscles. Hold for a brief count before returning to child pose on ankles...

8. Hip Fire Hydrants

Assume a quadruped position with toes pointing up (dorsiflexed). Lift from the hip, straight out, keeping the pelvis as flat as possible. Squeeze your glute at the top of the movement and return to the start position. Perform 5 – 10 reps on one side then switch to other side and repeat…

9. Striders With Rotation

Roughly assume a push / press up position and bring one foot down flat next to your hand. Drop your hips and rotate away from the outstretched foot. Return to the start position and repeat on the other side for a total of 5 – 10 reps each side…

10. Mountain Climbers

Again start in a push up position and drive one knee at a time towards your chest. Be dynamic with this movement for 10 – 20 reps each leg…

So there you have three basic warm ups which, when done one after the other, take approximately twelve minutes to complete properly.

Of course, if time is an issue then it's okay to pick one or two of them rather than all three, but when completed fully you'll find yourself slightly out of breath and lightly sweating.

Later on in this chapter I'll show you some more warm up examples you can use as you get more advanced but for now let's move on to a couple of example workouts!

Beginners 4-Week Full Body Program

Food Diary Template & Self-Check Information

Bedtime Last Night?

Did You Wake Feeling Refreshed?   Yes / No / Indifferent

What Time Did You Wake?

What Did You Have For Breakfast?

FOOD	FLUIDS	SUPPLEMENTS

Snack?

FOOD	FLUIDS	SUPPLEMENTS

What Did You Have For Lunch?

FOOD   FLUIDS   SUPPLEMENTS

Snack?

FOOD   FLUIDS   SUPPLEMENTS

What Did You Have For Dinner?

FOOD   FLUIDS   SUPPLEMENTS

Stress Levels Today? Poor / Average / Good

Energy Levels Today? Poor / Average / Good

Training Session Today? Poor / Average / Good

Not only does the food diary and self-check template give the athlete immediate feedback and a chance to improve certain lifestyle aspects (bedtime is always interesting) it gives me an indication as to how seriously an athlete is taking his or her programme.

The following diagram shows an example of how I was able to fit three training sessions into a goalkeeper's usual week. The goalkeeper in question was at university but came to me over the summer holidays, which is why I was able to schedule technical work and recovery into the programme. As we were able to get in recovery naps (summer holidays remember) week three was very hard training and week four was complete recovery...

Week 1 (Medium)	*Morning*	*Evening*
Sunday	Full Body 1	Hot & Cold Recovery
Monday	Goalkeeping Practice	
Tuesday	Goalkeeping Practice	Full Body 2
Wednesday	Massage Recovery	
Thursday	Goalkeeping Practice	Full Body 3
Friday	Swim Recovery	
Saturday	*Match*	Match warm down

Week 2 (Hard)	Morning	Evening
Sunday	Full Body 1	Hot & Cold Recovery
Monday	Goalkeeping Practice	Swim Recovery
Tuesday	Goalkeeping Practice	Full Body 2
Wednesday	Massage Recovery	
Thursday	Goalkeeping Practice	Full Body 3
Friday	Swim Recovery	
Saturday	*Match*	Match warm down

Week 3 (V. Hard)	Morning	Evening
Sunday	Full Body 1	Hot & Cold Recovery
Monday	Goalkeeping Practice	Massage Recovery
Tuesday	Goalkeeping Practice	Full Body 2
Wednesday	Goalkeeping Practice	Massage Recovery
Thursday	Goalkeeping Practice	Full Body 3
Friday	Goalkeeping Practice	
Saturday	*Match*	Match warm down

Week 4 (Recovery)	Morning	Evening
Sunday	Long Walk	Hot & Cold Recovery
Monday	Goalkeeping Practice	
Tuesday	Goalkeeping Practice	Light Sprints
Wednesday	Massage Recovery	
Thursday	Goalkeeping Practice	3-5km Jog with Stretch
Friday	Goalkeeping Practice	
Saturday	*Match*	Match warm down

The exercise programs were as follows, but bear in mind that the goalkeeper in question was completely new to this type of training (although he had some gym experience).

His movement patterns were quite good but not quite up to heavily loaded lifts just yet, so you'll see that the majority of the programme concentrated on bodyweight movements. He also followed the three warm ups previously shown in this chapter…

Full Body 1

1 – Box Jumps: 4 sets x 4-6 reps

2 – Sumo Deadlifts: 4-6 sets x 3-5 reps

3a – Press / Push Ups: 3-4 sets x AMRAP*

3b – Recline Rows: 3-4 sets x AMRAP*

3c – SB Rollouts: 3-4 sets x 12-15 reps

Full Body 2

1 – Med Ball Throw: 4 sets x 4-6 reps

2 – Military Press: 4-6 sets x 6-8 reps

3a – Walking Lunges: 3-4 sets x 6-8 reps each side

3b – Single Arm Kettlebell Rows: 3-4 sets x 8-12 reps each side

3c – Russian Twists: 3-4 sets x 12-20 reps each side

Full Body 3

1 – Kettlebell Swings: 4 sets x 6-8 reps (explosively)

2 – Goblet Squat: 4-6 sets x 8-12 reps

3a – Pull Ups: 3-4 sets x AMRAP*

3b – Hindu Press / Push Ups: 3-4 sets x AMRAP*

3c – SB Plank: 3-4 sets x 30-60 seconds

*AMRAP = As many repetitions as possible with good technique; stop as soon as

technique breaks down, preferably a repetition or two before!

Obviously I have no idea if you are familiar with these exercises or not, so let's run through a brief description of them alongside some action pictures…

Box Jumps

Exactly what it says on the tin – a jump onto a box (or something similar). This jump is a full body movement so start in front of a box with arms straight up above your head. Very quickly squat whilst simultaneously driving arms down and then up again as you launch upwards onto the top of the box. Land softly, get back down carefully and repeat. Don't make the mistake of trying to jump too high too soon. Technique is very important…

Sumo Deadlifts

Stand close to a loaded barbell with a wide stance. Hinge from the hips and reach for the barbell taking an alternate grip inside your stance. Pull the hips down, get your shoulders back and build tension through the body from the ground up. Drive the feet through the floor and pull the barbell up and back as you drive your hips forward. Slowly lower the bar and repeat…

Press / Push Ups

I'm hoping that you ran through the earlier movement pattern, going through the tutorial there. Just to recap though, get into a long body position with hands a shoulder-width apart with elbows turned in towards the body. Whilst completely tight, lower under control, pause at the bottom, then drive to the start / end position. Repeat as required…

Recline Rows

Again, reclines were covered in the movement pattern section but to recap - lie under a barbell and reach up with a just outside shoulder-width grip. Keep the body straight and tensed then pull your shoulders and elbows backwards until your chest hits the bar. Pause slightly then lower under control. Repeat for desired repetitions…

SB Rollouts

Kneel behind a Swiss/stability ball with hands just behind the top of ball. As you roll the ball forward travel forward on your knees. It's very important that you don't allow your hips to sag as you lengthen your body. Pull back with your abdominals to the start position and repeat for desired repetitions…

Med Ball Throw

I love this exercise and usually do it outside for height and distance. Take a light medicine ball and hold it in front of your chest. Squat and explode upwards throwing the ball from the chest with both hands outwards and up. Repeat for desired repetitions…

Military Press

Rest a loaded barbell across your collarbone with a shoulder width grip. Keep the body tight and drive the barbell up over your head. *DO NOT* lean back! Return to the start position and repeat for all repetitions…

Walking Lunges

Can be done with or without load, but in this example we are going to grab a pair of kettlebells or dumbbells and hold them by our sides. Take a big step forward and drop your rear knee towards the floor (but not on it!). Drive through the front foot and step forward as you lunge in alternate travelling fashion. Repeat for desired repetitions…

Single Arm Kettlebell Rows

Take a split stance holding one kettlebell or dumbbell if you prefer. Bend forward and tighten your body, holding back in a neutral position. Pull the elbow and shoulder back in a sawing / rowing motion. Pause at the top as you squeeze your back and return to start position. Repeat on both sides for desired repetitions…

Russian Twists

Assume a sit up position with a medicine or slam ball in front of your chest. Lift your feet off the floor and rotate from side to side at speed. Repeat for the desired number of repetitions…

Kettlebell Swings

Stand behind a heavy kettlebell and hinge forward from the hips as you take a grip on the 'bell. Pull the kettlebell back towards your lap and then drive the hips forward explosively whilst keeping a tight grip on the kettlebell handle. Allow the 'bell to swing back and then repeat for desired repetitions…

Goblet Squat

Take a heavy kettlebell and hold it under your chin just like you would if you were going to drink from a goblet. Sit down and back as you drive your knees outwards. Pause slightly at the bottom and drive upwards to the start position, repeating for desired repetitions…

Pull Ups

Take a just outside shoulder-width grip with palms facing away. Pull up and slightly back through your shoulders and elbows, driving your chest to the bar overhead. *DO NOT SWING UP!* This isn't a Cross Fit session. Keep technique tight throughout and repeat for as many good repetitions as possible…

Hindu Press / Push Ups

Currently my favourite push up variation, where you start with your body in an A-Frame position. Keeping your elbows in close to your body, slide your chest down and along the floor before performing a big back extension. Pause slightly; return to the start position to repeat for as many good repetitions as possible…

SB Plank

Just like a floor-based plank keep the body long and aligned but in this version your forearms are placed on top of a Swiss ball. Hold as still as possible (the closer your feet are together the harder the exercise) for the desired time…

Intermediate 4-Week Full Body Programme

The following training programme is one I prescribed for a slightly more advanced athlete who had been training with me for almost one year. I wouldn't allow any athlete to start here unless their movement patterns were very good and they had had some experience with these lifts previously.

For a warm up the athlete followed the previous examples plus one or all of the following dynamic movements…

Intermediate and Advanced Dynamic Warm Up

Round One

- High Knee Run in Place x 10 seconds
- Drop and Hold x 10 seconds
- Wide Outs x 10 seconds
- Drop and Hold x 10 seconds

Repeat straight through for two or three circuits…

High Knee Run

Effectively a sprint without moving anywhere, drive from the shoulders and get knees as high as possible whilst moving extremely quickly…

Drop and Hold

Drop into in half squat position and hold still. *DO NOT* place hands on thighs…

Wide Outs

In the half squat position jump feet out wide and then bring immediately back to start position. Keep head level and *DO NOT* stand upright during this exercise…

Round Two

- Low Skip
- High Knee Run Forwards
- Butt Kick
- High Knee Run Backwards
- Lateral Steps (left and right)
- Carioca (left and right)
- High Skip

(These movements are performed for distance. In my case the length available in the gym, but we also will go outside, mark off an area and usually work across varying distances).

Straight through for one or two circuits…

Low Skip

Basically time to remember playtime at school. A nice, light, gentle skip, not generating much force off the ground. Make sure to swing arms from shoulders…

High Knee Run (Forwards)

Just like the run in place but this time you travel forwards slowly instead of staying on the same spot…

Butt Kick

Whilst travelling, you flick your heels up towards your buttocks *BUT* in this version make sure your knees are lifted as well – this is much more like a normal running pattern, so carries over superbly well…

High Knee Run (Backwards)

As the forward version *BUT* travelling backwards…

Lateral Steps (Left and Right)

Crouch a little and then shuffle sideways to the left. *DO NOT* allow your feet to cross and then repeat to the right…

Carioca (Left and Right)

Same setup as lateral steps although this time you are crossing your feet in front and then behind behind you as you travel first one way, then the other…

Chapter 7

High Skip

Exactly like the previous skip but now trying for maximum distance and height…

Round Three

- Two Feet in Box
- One Foot in Box
- Two Feet in Sideways Box
- Hopscotch
- Slalom
- Ali Shuffle

Perform in an Agility Ladder for one to three circuits or repeated for a set time…

Two Feet in Box

Pretty much a high knee run performed through the ladder whereby both feet touch down in each box. As with all these agility drills start slow and increase speed as you gain confidence. Make sure that your arm swing comes from your shoulders to replicate running mechanics…

One Foot in Box

As you've probably guessed, just like the previous example except instead of both feet touching down in a single box, this time just one foot does...

Two Feet in Sideways Box

Stand side on to the ladder and move laterally making sure your running mechanics are good and both feet place in each box…

Hopscotch

Begin with feet and arms either side of ladder and simply jump in and out whilst travelling the length of the ladder…

Slalom

Probably the hardest of the movements to get right; you basically shuffle side to side across the ladder whilst simultaneously moving forward. The key to success here is to make sure that you start the movement with a step forward in the ladder, that way you are always moving up the ladder…

Ali Shuffle

Stand side on to the ladder and, just like the great man himself, shuffle your feet forwards and backwards whilst moving laterally along the ladder…

You now have a good few warm up drills in your toolbox. The key with the proper selection is to have a think about what your immediate requirements are. If you happen to be very tight then perform more SMR and floor-based dynamic mat work.

Should you lack a little agility then up the ladder drills. You could even take it a step further and catch a tennis or golf ball whilst performing them – the list really is endless.

What I don't want any of you to do is get too hot and bothered about what warm ups you should or shouldn't be doing. Ideally the warm up should flow seamlessly into the actual training programme. Don't look at a warm up as something separate. The very best athletes in the world are very serious about all they do – that's why they are at the top. Elite strength coach Dan John once said, "The warm up is the workout."

Let's now have a look at the intermediate programme with exercise descriptions and pictures…

Full Body 1

1 – Turkish Get Ups: 2-3 sets x 1-3 reps

2a – Box Squats: 4-6 sets x 3-5 reps

2b – Box Jumps: 4-6 sets x 1-3 reps

3a – KB Clean & Press: 3-4 sets x 6 reps

3b – Bent Over Rows: 3-4 sets x 8 reps

3c – Hanging Knee Raise: 3-4 sets x 12-20 reps

Full Body 2

1 – Deadlifts: 4-6 sets x 3-5 reps

2a – Bench Press: 3-5 sets x 4-6 reps

2b – Overhead Ball Slams: 3-5 sets x 1-3 reps

3a – Chin Ups: 3-4 sets x 6-8 reps (load if too easy)

3b – S/A KB Swings: 3-4 sets x 8 reps each

3c – Side Plank: 3-4 sets x 20-30 seconds each side

Full Body 3

1 – Hang Cleans: 4-6 sets x 3-5 reps

2 – Bulgarian (Raised) Split Squat: 4-5 sets x 5-8 reps each

3a – S/A KB Snatch: 3-4 sets x 6 reps each

3b – BB Push Press: 3-4 sets x 8 reps

3c – SB Prone Jacknife: 3-4 sets x 12-20 reps

Turkish Get Ups

I love this exercise due to its ability to utilise pretty much every muscle in the body. Lay flat with a moderately heavy kettlebell held straight up. If you are using your right hand bend your right knee and keep the other leg straight. Reverse this when you do the left side! You can really chunk this exercise down into four main movements.

1. Put your left arm out to the side and, keeping the kettlebell straight up at its highest point at all times, roll up into a sitting position.
2. From here drive the hips as high as you can and pause slightly.
3. Sweep the left leg back, under the body and behind you place the knee down on the floor – lift your left hand off the floor and make sure the whole body faces forward. You should now be in the bottom of a lunge position.
4. Driving from the front (right) foot stand as tall as possible. Now reverse the movement to get down…

Box Squats

My favourite squat (and the first barbell squat I always teach) for a number of reasons - notably with the box the depth that you squat is never in doubt. If I want you to squat to just below parallel I set the box to just below parallel and you hit it every time. It also is the easiest to teach, as you have to get your hips back and down to hit the box.

So, place a bar across your upper traps, stand in front of the box with a wide stance and sit down and back onto the box pushing knees out wide. Rest for a second or two then drive your traps through the bar as you stand up...

Box Jumps

After your squats, rest for no more than 15-20 seconds, then perform the box jumps exactly as you did in your earlier programme. This type of training is called *Contrast Training,* where you perform two similar movements (the second one being highly explosive) and is a highly effective form of training…

KB Clean & Press

Address a pair of moderately heavy kettlebells as if you were going to swing them but, as you start to swing them up - drive the hands quickly back under the 'bells and (in one movement) ad bring them to a rest in front of the chest (known as the rack position). From here push them up straight above your head and slightly together. Drop them back down under control to the rack position and allow the 'bells to swing back to start position. Repeat for desired repetitions…

Bent Over Rows

Take a barbell and hinge / bend forward from the hips (the clue is in the title, right?) and make sure that your whole body is tensed. You are going to pull the barbell back and up into the belly button region. Feel like you are pulling back with your elbows and make sure that you pause in the fully contracted position for a second. A big mistake I see here is people going too heavy with the load and not being able to keep a fully hinged body position or perform a slight pause…

Chapter 7

Hanging Knee Raise

Hang from a chinning bar and fighting the urge to swing, pull the knees up towards your chest. Hold in the top position and then return, under control, to the start position. Please note that I am quite tall and the bar wasn't high enough to allow me to hang with legs fully straight…

Deadlifts

Similar movement to the Sumo version in the beginner's programme but now we perform a more 'traditional' deadlift. Address the bar with your feet a comfortable distance apart. Hinge from the hips and take an alternate grip on the bar and pull your hips down, chest high and shoulders back. Create tension from the floor up and drive the feet through the floor as you lift the hips and shoulders at the same time. Finish the movement by 'popping' the hips through...

Bench Press

Lay back on a flat bench with feet 'tucked' as close to your buttocks as you can *WITHOUT* excessively arching your back. Take a shoulder-width grip (I'm not a fan of too wide a grip) of the bar and as you start the descent pinch your shoulder blades together. You want to feel like you are rowing the bar down to your chest rather than just allowing it to drop. Pause slightly at your nipple line and then drive the bar back to the start point...

Ball Slams

Combined with the Bench Press, in another example of contrast training, stand upright with ball held over your head. If you are using a med ball instead of a slam ball be very careful of the bounce! Just like you do a 'throw in' in football, explosively throw / slam the ball down into the ground…

Chapter 7

Chin Ups

Performed exactly like the earlier pullups, except your palms now face you in the classic chin up position. You can experiment with different width grips on each set should you want…

S/A KB Swings

As you've probably guessed, identical to the double handed swing except single-handed. The only thing I change is to turn the hand inward to lessen the strain on the biceps. Perform all reps on one side then repeat on the other...

Side Plank

Lay on your side with your elbow *DIRECTLY* under your shoulder. Drive your hips high off the floor and hold that alignment for the allotted time. Repeat for the same time on the other side…

Hang Cleans

A big hip extension exercise, take the barbell and stand with it in front of thighs (hang position). Hinge from the hips (hip flexion) and let the barbell drift down towards your knees. Bring hips forward (hip extension), slowly at first, keeping your weight back in your heels. As the barbell approaches your hips explode the rest of the way forward; shrug your shoulders and pull the barbell up. Catch the barbell on your collarbone; allow your elbows to travel as far forward as possible.

Bulgarian (Raised) Split Squat

Even though I have been in the gym environment for over 30 years now, no one can tell me why this exercise is forever known as the 'Bulgarian' split squat. It's certainly not known by that name in Bulgaria!

Raise the back foot on a bench or step (not too high) with other foot out in front. Use your body weight or if too easy hold dumbbells or kettlebells in your hands. Slowly sink down and back until your back knee is just above the floor. Pause for a second then drive through the front foot and return to start position. When done switch to the other side for desired repetitions…

S/A KB Snatch

A very explosive exercise which starts off as a single arm kettlebell swing but as you raise the 'bell you want to pull it onto the back of the wrist as you punch hard towards the ceiling, all in one movement. You'll know when this is done correctly as you will hardly feel the movement of the kettlebell. Perform on each side for the desired repetitions…

BB Push Press

A much more explosive version of the strict overhead press in which power is generated by performing a very small squat and then exploding upwards with the barbell. You will discover, as a result, you will be able to press more weight with this exercise. A common mistake sees athletes bend their knees to generate the push instead of sitting back into their hips as per a full squat…

SB Prone Jacknife

Assume a push / press up position with feet balanced on a Swiss ball. Keeping your body as still and flat as possible pull your knees (and the ball) in towards your chest. Return the ball to start position and repeat for desired repetitions…

Advanced 4-Week Full Body Programme

This programme was given to a goalkeeper who had been training with me for a good eighteen months and who had built a considerable amount of strength in that time.

He was also very technically efficient with all the movements and most importantly had a really good recovery programme in place!

Please don't be fooled by the apparent simplicity of this programme. If you have trained hard up to this point (and I really hope you have) these programmes will be difficult at best.

Full Body 1

1 – Turkish Get Ups and Windmill: 2-3 sets x 1-3 reps

2a – Cleans: 4-6 sets x 3-5 reps

2b – Front Squats: 4-6 sets x 6-8 reps

3a – Lateral Step Ups: 3-4 sets x 6 reps

3b – Mixed Grip Chins: 3-4 sets x 8 reps

Full Body 2

1 – Snatch Grip Deadlift: 4-6 sets x 2-5 reps

2a – Incline Bench Press: 4-6 sets x 5-8 reps

2b – Clapping Push / Press Ups: 4-6 sets x 2-5 reps

3a – SB Hip Extension & Leg Curl: 3-4 sets x 8-12 reps

3b – Battling Ropes: 3-4 sets x 20-30 seconds

Full Body 3

1 – Double Kettlebell Snatch: 3-4 sets x 3-6 reps

2 – DB Squat into Box Jump: 4-6 sets x 3-5 reps

3a – BB Split Jerk: 3-4 sets x 6 reps

3b – Cheat Curls: 3-4 sets x 6-8 reps

3c – SB Crunches: 3-4 sets x 12-20 reps

Turkish Get Ups and Windmill

Perform a get up, as before, and in the fully standing position turn your feet away from the kettlebell. This movement is made possible by you pushing your hips back towards the 'bell as you bend and slightly rotate, reaching towards the floor. Keeping your abdominals tight, come up and 'pop' the hips back into the starting position. Repeat on both sides for the desired number of repetitions…

Cleans

The full movement starts exactly like a deadlift then explodes from the hips just like the hang clean. As you shrug and pull the barbell up, you want to drop underneath it extremely quickly and catch the bar on your collarbone then stand. Return to the start and repeat for desired repetitions...

Front Squats

If you look at the previous two pictures they depict a perfect front squat! Hold a barbell across your collarbone with elbows pushed through. Keeping your trunk as upright as possible sit back and down forcing your knees out wide. Squat low and drive back to your starting position then repeat for desired repetitions…

Lateral Step Ups

Stand side on to a bench or step, with the inside foot up. Making sure that your knee doesn't fall inwards as you stand tall, pause for a second or two and lower slowly. Repeat, then switch sides for desired repetitions. Holding a dumbbell in the outside hand will make the exercise more challenging...

Mixed Grip Chins

Performed exactly the same way as the previous examples except that one hand has palms facing away, and the other has palms facing towards you. Perform all the repetitions with this grip then change the hands and perform the same number of repetitions…

Snatch Grip Deadlift

This more difficult version of the traditional deadlift requires not only a wide grip on the barbell but a good degree of mobility and flexibility to perform whilst maintaining good technique…

Incline Bench Press

No different to the earlier bench press *EXCEPT* that instead of the bench being flat you incline it slightly. Be mindful that the higher the incline of the bench the more you shift the focus from the chest to the shoulders...

Clapping Push / Press Ups

A highly explosive push up that has you clapping at the top of the push movement then catching the downward drop before exploding back into another repetition. Although there are guidelines for repetitions I often stop the exercise as soon as the power leaves the movement...

SB Hip Extension & Leg Curl

A great movement that works the hamstrings through both flexion and extension. Lay on your back with your feet on top of a Swiss ball. Drive the hips up, squeeze your glutes, and pull the ball in towards your bum. Hold the contraction in your glutes and hamstrings before returning the ball. Repeat for desired repetitions…

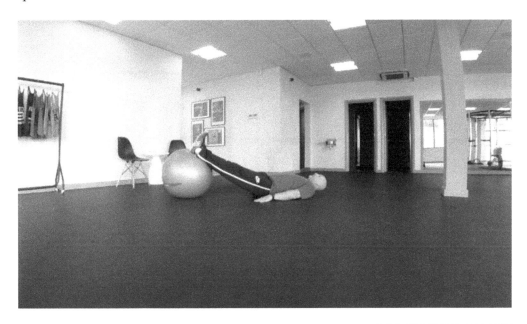

Chapter 7

Battling Ropes

How much fun can you have with a big heavy rope! Secure the loop and grab the ends of the rope. Make sure you have plenty of slack in the rope and take a relaxed athletic stance. Vigorously snap your arms up and down aiming to get a snake like effect with the rope. Usually performed for time this is a lot harder than it looks…

Double Kettlebell Snatch

Performed in exactly the same way as the single kettlebell version except, you've got it, you use two kettlebells. You'll need to go lighter than you think with this version…

DB Squat into Box Jump

Hold a pair of heavy dumbbells by your side just behind a high box. Perform a full squat then, as you begin to drop into a second one, let go of the dumbbells and explode up onto the box. Repeat for desired repetitions…

BB Split Jerk

An extremely explosive overhead press which is timed with a big split forward and backwards of the legs. Make sure you keep changing which leg you go forward with every repetition…

Cheat Curls

To all intents and purposes a reverse-grip hang clean. So use a big hip extension to allow you to curl a much heavier weight than you normally would. Control the bar back to the start position. Be careful not to lean back as you pull the weight up…

SB Crunches

Effectively a crunch performed whilst lying over a Swiss ball. The advantage of this is you are able to really stretch the abdominals before every repetition. Be controlled with every rep and make sure you force all the air out of your chest as you roll up…

So there you have typical beginner, intermediate and advanced level training programmes. One thing I need to make very clear is that the best training programme in the world won't be at all effective if the amount of effort you put in is patchy.

In fact I'd go one better and say that the athlete who is on the worst programme, but attacks it with everything they've got on a consistent basis, will always get better results than the athlete that just plays around with a much better programme.

It always boils down to you, your commitment, and how hard you're prepared to work on a consistent basis. Never forget that!

Some of the best results I've ever seen have come from using very basic equipment (barbell, Olympic plates, couple of kettlebells and a chin up bar) using basic movement patterns and a commitment to keep improving and moving forward.

The best usually become the best because they work the hardest!

Good luck…

8
FAQs

Why do you have some exercises numbered 1 and others 2a, 2b, etc.?

That's a great question and simple to answer. When you see a number like 1 for example, with no letter following immediately, you perform one set of that exercise, rest, then perform another until all sets have been completed.

When you see 2a and 2b, however, perform one set of exercise 2a, pause briefly then complete one set of exercise 2b. Rest, then repeat for the designated number of sets. This is known as a superset.

The same is true if you see three of the same number, which is called a tri-set.

How much rest should I have between sets?

This is going to depend on a lot of factors, but let's keep it really simple. Try not to rest for any longer than 60-90 seconds between each set.

It's true to say that when you start to lift very heavy weights it does place heavy demands on your central nervous system. Usually this requires more time to recover between sets and you may see elite weightlifters rest for up to 6 minutes between sets for this very reason!

However, most elite sports don't give you the luxury of a long rest between periods of explosive activity, so for that very reason I prefer a much shorter recovery time.

Chapter 8

What is the best way to progress from workout to workout?

The truthful answer to a very good question is that there is no best way –
everyone will progress at different rates. But, with that said and done, this is an
example of how I'd progress someone through the first beginner's programme…

The first exercise in the programme is Box Jumps, which requires the athlete to
perform four total sets of between 4-6 repetitions. I would aim to get the height of
the box such that it was a tough 4 reps.

The next week I would try to hit 5 reps at the same height. As soon as 6 reps were
completed I would raise the height of the box and drop to 4 reps again.

I would follow the same pattern throughout the programme. For instance, during
the sumo deadlifts that follow, I'd have the athlete perform four sets of 3-5 reps
the first week, five sets of 3-5 reps on week two, and aim for six sets on the third
week. Week four I'd drop a couple of sets and back off.

All it takes is a little thought and common sense.

*The workouts you've provided seem quite brief – don't you have to train for
longer to get better results?*

There's an old saying that goes something like… "You can train hard, or you can
train long. But you can't train hard and long!" And that sums it up really well.
I'm not really a clock-watcher in the gym (except when manipulating rest
periods) but rarely does an athlete train for over an hour with me.

The point to understand is that your strength sessions are here to ultimately
enhance your ability as a goalkeeper, *NOT* leave you so sore for days afterwards
that you are unable to do your skill work or play.

A hot topic at the moment is player recovery. Just how much rest should a player
receive between matches? For me it all boils down to one simple outcome…

All that training, nutrition, rest and recovery MUST result in making sure the
player is able to perform at their highest level come match day.

The best training programme in the world is useless if it leaves the player too 'tired' to play!

There doesn't seem to be much focused core work in your programmes – will I have to add it in?

I really find people's fascination with 'core training' and the chasing of a six-pack difficult to fathom. As I remind people constantly, an athlete has a six-pack usually as a result of the training/performing they do, they don't have a six-pack then become an athlete.

Quality strength training, which covers all our natural movement patterns will get your core extremely strong and cross over very well to your athletic movements.

That said I do include a few rotation, anti-rotation, roll out movements, which could be described as direct core exercises.

I don't like squatting or deadlifting – what should I do instead?

A different training programme!

If I wanted to add some extra arm work into the programme, could I?

Well, my question to you would be… "Why?" Do you believe that bigger 'guns' will make you a better goalkeeper or do you just want to show them off on the training ground?

The fact remains that my job is to get the athlete that hires me as strong, powerful, explosive, and as lean as possible. Don't think that just because there aren't half a dozen different arm exercises in the programme your biceps and triceps won't get enough stimulation. Don't think like a bodybuilder. Concentrate on becoming the best athlete you can be.

Chapter 8

Will I get too big doing this programme?

That's a very good and valid question, one that I'm asked all the time especially by female athletes. To be honest this is also a difficult question to answer because the amount of muscle someone will put on is very much an individual thing.

Firstly, don't worry if you're female. It takes years and years of training, lots of eating and the manipulation of hormones for you to put any appreciable muscle on.

For you guys the water is slightly more muddy. If you are doing lots of technical work, plenty of fitness and conditioning then realistically you're not going to be putting slabs of muscle onto your physique.

Ultimately if you train like a bodybuilder with high frequency and volume then you are likely to increase the sarcoplasm (fluid) around your muscle fibres leading to an increase in the size of your muscles. This serves bodybuilders well but as 'non-functional' muscle won't really do much for your athleticism.

Correct strength training however increases myofibrillar density, which simply refers to the density of the actual muscle (how many fibres are packed in there).

With more muscle fibre comes the potential of a bigger signal from the central nervous system enabling an increased expression of strength. In other words you may get slightly bigger but it will only enhance your ability as a fast, explosive and highly powerful athlete.

As a vegan, will I be able to cope with all the training and recover well?

Another great question to which the answer is yes, of course you will. History is littered with champions who have taken animal products out of their lives. The only point I'd make here is make sure that you get all of your nutrients on board.

You are certainly going to have to plan your meals with a lot of thought as lots of vegans I've worked with sometimes have to watch out for an essential fat deficiency – this is something to bear in mind.

Is it better to lift weights in the morning or later on in the day?

Plenty of research has been done on this very subject and it's believed that late morning or early afternoon is probably the time when you are at your strongest. That said if you can only lift first thing in the morning or last thing at night then get on with it.

How many hours of sleep are ideal?

Research in this very area is actually quite inconclusive and really does depend on a variety of factors, but what does seem important is the quality of sleep.

With that in mind I'd set your room up to support a fantastic night's sleep; go to bed at a reasonable hour and see what time you wake up in the morning.

A full and restful sleep should have you up and refreshed every single day even if you need an alarm call to get up.

How long should a gut healing protocol last for?

This is a simple question to answer and it relates to all things health… forever! The more steps you take to promote health and wellbeing the better your body will respond to any stimulus (including training) you put it under.

The missing link when dealing with any training programme, whether it's to build muscle, burn body fat, or indeed get stronger, is the health of the participant. Get that right and the rest is just detail…

What should I do when I've gone through all the included training programmes?

Firstly please understand that the programmes included in this book are examples of the programmes I'm currently running with the athletes I'm training.

As a result they are a lot more generic than I would like, although they are still extremely effective. You will always get better results with a programme that has been designed specifically for you, the individual, but I'm very well aware that this isn't always possible.

There is always a fine line to be trodden when writing exercise programmes for a group of athletes, so I usually start with a general programme and make small changes depending on the level of the athlete. That way I don't have to write twenty different programmes if I have a group of twenty athletes in at one time.

You should always be looking at every programme that you have access to with that 'individual' mindset. That way you can tweak the programme so it suits you more. By all means contact me and I'll gladly supply you with more training programmes or help individualise the ones you have.

I've seen a lot of training videos on YouTube where athletes are lifting with the use of bands and chains – why do you not show this in your included programmes?

The use of adding chains and resistance bands to a barbell or other equipment is known as 'accommodating resistance'. Effectively they are a method of working with an athlete's natural strength curve, overcoming any sticking points and rapidly increasing an athlete's strength.

Let's say, for example, you perform a bench press with additional chains on the bar. When you unload the bar and hold it at the fully extended part of the lift you are at your strongest. Here the chains are unravelled from the floor and adding their most resistance to the load.

As you bring the bar down to your chest you are actually moving towards the weakest part of the lift and the chains collect on the floor lightening the load.

As you press, the load increases as the chains unravel which has the effect of enhancing your natural strength curve. In theory this is brilliant *BUT* in my opinion is for advanced athletes only. You need a good foundation of strength *BEFORE* you start thinking of adding advanced tools.

A couple of times during the book you mention the right 'environment' for success. Can you explain exactly what you mean?

There are always going to be situations in life over which you have no control - other than how you respond to them.

There are, however, many situations that you can have influence, or be influenced by. Take the gym you train in, for example. Is it truly aligned with your goal of becoming the best athlete/goalkeeper you can be?

Over the years I've been in some fantastic facilities, which are set up in such a way as to immediately increase your personal best lifts just by walking through the front door.

Gyms which blast music from every corner, smell of ammonia and chalk dust, gyms where you can hear weight plates slam together and feel the vibration of dumbbells and barbells hitting the floor constantly. Gyms where all the people present have just one goal in mind – *to be the best they can be…*

Then you have the other gyms. I'm sorry to say there are now gyms throughout the world that won't let you use chalk. They won't let you perform certain exercises like deadlifts because they deem them dangerous. They frown upon you making any noise and unbelievably then make you slow down if you start to sweat.

You do not want to be training in these gyms. That is not the correct environment for success. I spoke recently to a young footballer about this very thing. He wanted to train at the same gym as all his friends. It wasn't the right environment for him to pursue his own goal.

Your goal is your goal, no one else's. Make sure you do all you can to help make that dream a reality!

When do you consider someone grounded enough in the basics and ready for more challenging exercises and loads?

How long's a piece of string really?

This is a great question and depends on many different factors. If I'm honest with you I never really come too far away from the basics, even with the most

207

advanced athletes.

Firstly, I want to make sure the athlete has a good understanding of the primal patterns. This means he or she can push, pull, squat, lunge, hinge/bend, rotate and perform on a single leg without restriction. This is fundamentally important. From there I work to improve these patterns and increase his or her athleticism with gymnastic type drills. At the same time I like to place a focus on exercises such as squats, deadlifts, military presses, KB swings, DB/KB clean and presses, DB/KB snatches, loaded carries such as farmers walks, press/push ups, chin/pull ups, and where possible rope climbs and sled drags and pushes.

That doesn't mean I don't give an athlete other exercises to perform, it just means that, in my opinion, the further you move away from these basics the slower your overall progress will be.

You make reference during the book to training with tyres, sleds and barrels yet none of them are in the training programmes. Why is this?

Quite simply, very few gyms carry this type of equipment. There are more 'warehouse' type gyms around these days but the majority throw in this advanced training kit with no real knowledge (other than what they see on YouTube) as how to best use it.

The idea with this particular book was to give everyone who reads it the opportunity of performing the exercise programmes included. If I added tyres, kegs and sleds that could make it very difficult for many readers to follow.

Graduation: Life Lessons of a Professional Footballer by Richard Lee

The 2010/11 season will go down as a memorable one for Goalkeeper Richard Lee. Cup wins, penalty saves, hypnotherapy and injury would follow, but these things only tell a small part of the tale. Filled with anecdotes, insights, humour and honesty - Graduation uncovers Richard's campaign to take back the number one spot, save a lot of penalties, and overcome new challenges. What we see is a transformation - beautifully encapsulated in this extraordinary season.

"Whatever level you have played the beautiful game and whether a goalkeeper or outfield player, you will connect with this book. Richard's honesty exposes the fragility in us all, he gives an honest insight into dimensions of a footballer's life that are often kept a secret and in doing so offers worthy advice on how to overcome any hurdle. A great read." **Ben Foster, Goalkeeper, West Bromwich Albion & England.**

Soccer Tough by Dan Abrahams

"Take a minute to slip into the mind of one of the world's greatest soccer players and imagine a stadium around you. Picture a performance under the lights and mentally play the perfect game."

Technique, speed and tactical execution are crucial components of winning soccer, but it is mental toughness that marks out the very best players – the ability to play when pressure is highest, the opposition is strongest, and fear is greatest. Top players and coaches understand the importance of sport psychology in soccer but how do you actually train your mind to become the best player you can be?

Soccer Tough demystifies this crucial side of the game and offers practical techniques that will enable soccer players of all abilities to actively develop focus, energy, and confidence. Soccer Tough will help banish the fear, mistakes, and mental limits that holds players back.

Scientific Approaches to Goalkeeping in Football: A practical perspective on the most unique position in sport
by Andy Elleray

Do you coach goalkeepers and want to help them realise their fullest potential? Are you a goalkeeper looking to reach the top of your game? Then search no further and dive into this dedicated goalkeeping resource. Written by goalkeeping guru Andy Elleray this book offers a fresh and innovative approach to goalkeeping in football. With a particular emphasis on the development of young goalkeepers, it sheds light on training, player development, match performances, and player analysis. Utilising his own experiences Andy shows the reader various approaches, systems and exercises that will enable goalkeepers to train effectively and appropriately to bring out the very best in them.

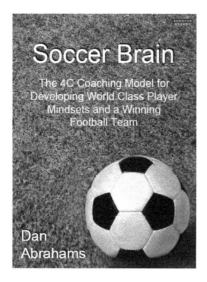

Soccer Brain: The 4C Coaching Model for Developing World Class Player Mindsets and a Winning Football Team
by Dan Abrahams

Coaching soccer is demanding. Impossible to perfect, it requires a broad knowledge of many performance areas including technique, tactics, psychology and the social aspects of human development. The first two components are covered in detail in many texts – but Soccer Brain uniquely offers a comprehensive guide to developing the latter two – player mindsets and winning teams.

Soccer Brain is for the no limits coach. It's for the coach who is passionate about developing players and building a winning team. This is not a traditional soccer coaching book filled with drills or tactics or playing patterns. This book is about getting the very best from you, the coach, and helping you develop a coaching culture of excellence and world class football mindsets.

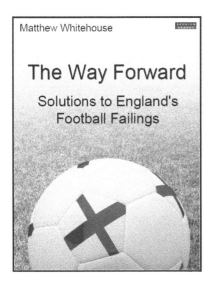

The Way Forward: Solutions to England's Football Failings
by Matthew Whitehouse

English football is in a state of crisis. It has been almost 50 years since England made the final of a major championship and the national sides, at all levels, continue to disappoint and underperform. Yet no-one appears to know how to improve the situation.

In his acclaimed book, The Way Forward, football coach Matthew Whitehouse examines the causes of English football's decline and offers a number of areas where change and improvement need to be implemented immediately. With a keen focus and passion for youth development and improved coaching he explains that no single fix can overcome current difficulties and that a multi-pronged strategy is needed. If we wish to improve the standards of players in England then we must address the issues in schools, the grassroots, and academies, as well as looking at the constraints of the Premier League and English FA.

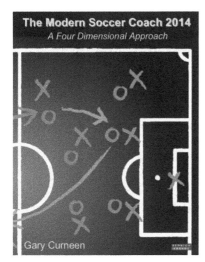

The Modern Soccer Coach by Gary Curneen

Aimed at Soccer coaches of all levels and with players of all ages and abilities The Modern Soccer Coach 2014 identifies the areas that must be targeted by coaches who want to maximize a team's potential – the Technical, Tactical, Physical, and Mental sides to the game.

See how the game has changed and what areas determine success in the game today. Learn what sets coaches like Mourinho, Klopp, Rodgers, and Guardiola apart from the rest. Philosophies and training methods from the most forward thinking coaches in the game today are presented, along with guidelines on creating a modern environment for readers' teams. This book is not about old school methodologies – it is about creating a culture of excellence that gets the very best from players. Contains more than 30 illustrated exercises that focus on tactical, technical, mental, and physical elements of the game.

José Mourinho: The Rise of the Translator by Ciaran Kelly

From Porto to Chelsea, and Inter to Real Madrid – the Mourinho story is as intriguing as the man himself. Now, a new challenge awaits at Stamford Bridge. Covering the Mourinho story to October 2013 and featuring numerous exclusive interviews with figures not synonymous with the traditional Mourinho narrative.

"Enlightening interviews with those who really know José Mourinho" – Simon Kuper, Financial Times.

"Superb read from a terrific writer" – Ger McCarthy, Irish Examiner

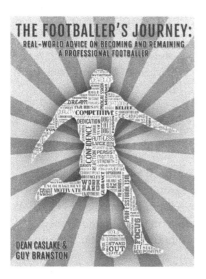

The Footballer's Journey: real-world advice on becoming and remaining a professional footballer by Dean Caslake and Guy Branston

Many youngsters dream of becoming a professional footballer. But football is a highly competitive world where only a handful will succeed. Many aspiring soccer players don't know exactly what to expect, or what is required, to make the transition from the amateur world to the 'bright lights' in front of thousands of fans.

The Footballer's Journey maps out the footballer's path with candid insight and no-nonsense advice. It examines the reality of becoming a footballer including the odds of 'making it', how academies really work, the importance of attitude and mindset, and even the value of having a backup plan if things don't quite work out. Filled with real life stories from current, and former, professionals across different leagues.

Lightning Source UK Ltd.
Milton Keynes UK
UKHW030606141019
351570UK00008B/604/P